Disaster Insurance Reimagined

Disaster Insurance Reimagined

Protection in a Time of Increasing Risk

Paula Jarzabkowski
Konstantinos Chalkias
Eugenia Cacciatori
and
Rebecca Bednarek

OXFORD
UNIVERSITY PRESS

OXFORD
UNIVERSITY PRESS

Great Clarendon Street, Oxford, OX2 6DP,
United Kingdom

Oxford University Press is a department of the University of Oxford.
It furthers the University's objective of excellence in research, scholarship,
and education by publishing worldwide. Oxford is a registered trade mark of
Oxford University Press in the UK and in certain other countries

Published in the United States of America by Oxford University Press
198 Madison Avenue, New York, NY 10016, United States of America

British Library Cataloguing in Publication Data
Data available

Library of Congress Control Number: 2023930293

ISBN 978-0-19-286516-8

DOI: 10.1093/oso/9780192865168.001.0001

Printed and bound by
CPI Group (UK) Ltd, Croydon, CR0 4YY

Links to third party websites are provided by Oxford in good faith and
for information only. Oxford disclaims any responsibility for the materials
contained in any third-party website referenced in this work.

Contents

List of figures, tables, and case examples

Figures

Tables

Case examples

Preface

When we started this project, we already knew how insurance and reinsurance markets work in trading disaster risk. This book follows on from a global ethnography of the reinsurance industry that started in 2009 and resulted in the publication of a book—*Making a Market for Acts of God*—in 2015. We continued to follow these markets as, strangely to our partners and friends, they fascinated us. We saw the increasing frequency and severity of disasters, even as the amount of uninsured economic loss post-disaster was also increasing. As the news showed country-after-country devastated by extreme flooding, hurricane, and wildfire, the (re)insurance markets we had studied were not always there to cover all, or even most of, the losses. Indeed, it seemed disaster insurance was under real strain.

Climate change, accompanied by increasing urbanization and geopolitical changes, is making policyholders, geographical areas, and even specific disasters uninsurable in the private insurance sector. We wanted to understand how the resultant insurance protection gaps (uninsured economic losses post-disaster) were being managed in different countries. This drew our attention to different entities around the world that operate between the government and the insurance industry to provide novel solutions to insurance protection gaps in their respective countries or regions. Curious to understand more about this global phenomenon, we started what became a global study of these "Protection Gap Entities" (PGEs); the entities that bring together different insurance, government, and intergovernmental stakeholders in efforts to address these insurance protection gap. Ultimately our study covered 17 of these PGEs operating across 49 countries. In this book we explain how PGEs come about, the work they do to make disasters insurable, and the opportunities and challenges they face as they evolve in a world of increasing disaster. We conclude by positioning them within a reimagined insurance landscape that has disaster protection at its heart.

In conducting this research, we moved between many different countries, organizations, and types of disasters. We sat in meetings about flood and terrorism risk in London, and on Organization for Economic Co-operation and Development (OECD) meetings about pandemic risk. We attended industry conferences in many countries, from Australia to South Africa to the USA, learning about the difficulties of insuring earthquakes, hurricanes, terrorist attacks, and droughts. We supported knowledge exchange, bringing three multi-country PGEs together to discuss their challenges and opportunities at the World Bank Understanding Risk conference in Mexico. We chaired the 2019 International Forum of Terrorism Risk (Re)Insurance Pools (IFTRIP) in person in Belgium and then virtually in the first year of the COVID-19 pandemic in 2020. We presented and discussed our findings in London, Madrid, Johannesburg, Paris, and Moscow, and to market, government, and other stakeholders. We sat in countless online calls with various backdrops, ranging from the hushed corporate boardroom of a European PGE, to the crowing of roosters at dawn in the Pacific islands, to urgent conversations with international aid experts on the way to an airport, to the unsurprisingly emotional talk with a government official in the Caribbean after a hurricane. All of these made us conscious of the significance of PGEs in the global landscape of disaster insurance but also revealed the vast variations in both the problems they are addressing and the solutions they provide.

Among these differences, which we cover in this book, we could not ignore two overarching commonalities. First, insurance is desperately needed. Whether this is government officials describing the difference that just US $10 million in insurance payments could make in disaster response. Or the palpable security that comes from knowing there is insurance to pay for rebuilding homes after a flood or restarting a business after a terrorist attack. Second, as the vast problem of insuring disaster grows, PGE managers are embracing wholeheartedly the challenges of building capability and capital to provide protection from the ever-increasing threat of disaster. During our research, the countries we studied, including our own, experienced droughts, flood, hurricanes, wildfires, terrorist attacks, volcanic eruptions, and earthquakes. We saw first-hand, in the context of the climate crisis and a pandemic, the difference it makes when insurance can be relied upon to help with recovery, and the additional devastation when it cannot. PGEs are not perfect, or a panacea, but they can and do make a difference in disaster recovery. Our passion has been to collect data on these organizations and the stakeholders that work with them, bear witness to the disasters they address and the challenges they face, and to support new ways of reimagining disaster insurance that can provide better protection for everyone.

Who should read this book?

- *Those interested in disasters, from climate change to financial collapse, and disaster insurance.* We explore the shifting disaster risk landscape for insurance in relation to the growing insurance protection gap globally. Extreme weather, terrorist attacks, and seismological disasters that move beyond the scope of the private insurance sector, herald the collapse of disaster insurance. This is important as insurance is a cornerstone of many modern economies. PGEs are increasingly important players in maintaining the continuity of disaster insurance. In this book, we offer provocative conclusions about the challenging future of disaster insurance, and the role of PGEs in it.

- *Those working for Protection Gap Entities (PGEs).* Our research study incorporates global breadth and variation as we studied 17 PGEs operating across 49 countries, employing different governance structures, and covering different types of disasters. As a result, the book offers managers who work for PGEs a comprehensive understanding of the similarities and differences, the opportunities and challenges, as well as the past, present, and future of PGEs within the global landscape of disaster insurance.

- *Professionals working on disaster risk management.* Our study provides a multi-stakeholder view of PGEs and their role in the disaster insurance landscape. As well as the PGEs, we talked with people from the *insurance industry* such as insurers, reinsurers, modelers, and brokers; *governments* such as ministers, treasury departments, environment agencies, and disaster management authorities; *intergovernmental organizations* such as the World Bank and OECD; and other key stakeholders such as *resilience and reconstruction* teams. Our book is valuable for these professionals in disaster risk management, explaining the role played by PGEs in helping manage disaster: for instance, the client manager in a reinsurance company that sees a potential commercial opportunity with a PGE, or a local government official wanting to address their community's repeated flooding issue, or a disaster risk manager in a humanitarian or development agency wanting to provide stable disaster relief financing to vulnerable populations after droughts, floods, and tropical storms. Reading this book, these professionals will understand how PGEs work and they will appreciate the wider ecosystem of different solutions, challenges, and approaches globally. They will also know more about how disaster insurance relates to physical resilience and how the two need to be integrated if we are to move to a more sustainable future.

- *Those interested in public-private partnerships and cross-sector collaborations.* This book presents the tensions and dynamics of collaborations between private sector, government, and intergovernmental stakeholders. The PGEs we explore in this book have varying governance structures ranging from fully private to government-owned, and involve different collaborative arrangements between public, private and civil society organizations. Such partnerships and collaborations are often considered controversial, prone to misplaced goals, and even to failure. Many of our PGEs do face challenges from the competing demands upon them. Nonetheless, they persist and play a critical role in continuing to offer disaster insurance where it would otherwise be unavailable. We offer the reader an opportunity to explore these complex collaborative arrangements further, understanding how they work, and the challenges involved.

- *Scholars interested in paradox.* We use paradox theory as a conceptual organizing device throughout the book. Paradox scholars can draw from our book to understand the paradoxical dynamics involved in addressing a grand societal challenge—how to maintain a disaster insurance system that is in crisis—between the different interests of the multiple organizations involved. It provides paradox scholars with an empirical example of how multiple paradoxes knot together and the dynamic interplay between equilibrium and disequilibrium as they become imbalanced. Rather than a conceptual work, our book offers rich empirical insights into how paradoxes play out in addressing real-world challenges and demonstrates the value of paradox theory as a lens for explaining these challenges.

- *Scholars interested in insurance and risk.* The book presents a rich empirical context and plenty of insights into the field of insurance and risk, particularly disaster insurance. We open the topic for those broadly interested in knowing how insurance works and exploring the role of insurance in societies. Our book presents a rare social science insight into the market for disaster risk that can complement actuarial, technical, or economic knowledge of how insurance works.

How to read this book

This book was written with a vision of someone reading it as a "journey" from cover to cover. However, if you want a quicker entry into the book's key insights you should first read the introduction before (hopefully) dipping into individual chapters. Each chapter focuses on a specific question, so you can read the chapter's introduction to decide which are of most interest to you: why do PGEs start (Chapter 2); how do they work (Chapter 3); how do they evolve with new risks (Chapter 4); can PGEs support physical resilience (Chapter 5); and what is the role of PGEs in reimagining disaster insurance (Chapter 6)? These should allow quick entry points into specific topics. At the end of each chapter, we also include key learning points that summarize the main implications.

While we have stripped out some of the technicality of insurance (a necessary step that will likely be noticeable to insurance professionals), some specific terminology is unavoidable. A comprehensive glossary is therefore provided. If you find a term puzzling, look to the glossary, where it should be explained. In addition, our Appendix material provides, first, an overview of the process of risk transfer (and the PGE intervention in it) for those less familiar with the insurance market and, second, the methods and dataset on which our book is based.

Throughout this book we refer to many PGEs by name and provide verbatim quotes from our data. We have, however, edited such quotes where necessary to make technical insurance or disaster terminology accessible to a wider audience, or to preserve the anonymity of the speaker.

Happy reading! We are passionate about this issue of disaster insurance and how to do it WELL in a world increasingly exposed to disasters. We also learnt so much from engaging with our research participants in so many different parts of the world (some multiple times over multiple years) and from writing this book together as a research team. We hope that shows in the pages that follow.

Acknowledgments

We are grateful to the many individuals from PGEs, development organizations, the insurance industry, government departments, and others who gave their time and insight to this project. You allowed us to see the challenges of, and solutions to, the insurance protection gap through your eyes. In your various ways, you were all committed to improving protection, ensuring people had money to respond to and recover from disaster. Yet you were also candid about the uncertainties and frustrations of trying to make the disaster insurance system work better. We would never have understood the complex dynamics of insuring the uninsurable in the face of increasing disaster without your candor and generosity. Thank you.

Special thanks are due to those of you in the PGEs we studied, who helped us with access, insights, and feedback on our emerging findings. Of these, Isaac Anthony, Andy Bord, Julian Enoizi, Francisco Espejo Gil, Martin Jordi, Danny Marshall, Alain Marti, Laurent Montador, Lesley Ndlovu, and Chris Wallace are due especial thanks for smoothing the path of our data collection, and repeatedly sharing their knowledge throughout the study. In addition, we are grateful to all the participants that granted us access to conduct our project.

We appreciate the funding received from different industry partners and institutions between 2016 and 2019 that enabled us to collect these data, including the Bank of England, Bayes Business School, City, University of London, Birkbeck, University of London, Pool Re, and Willis Towers Watson.

We are also grateful for the funding received from some PGEs, insurance industry partners, and institutions to support research assistance in the writing of this book from 2019 to 2021. We appreciate that these funds were given without conditions, control, or oversight over the content; thanks to Australian Reinsurance Pool Corporation (ARPC), Flood Re, Guy Carpenter, Hiscox, the International Forum of Terrorism Risk (Re)Insurance Pools (IFTRIP), the Leverhulme Trust, Pool Re, and Präventionsstiftung der Kantonalen Gebäudeversicherungen. We also acknowledge that this project has received funding from the European Union's Horizon 2020 research and innovation programme under grant agreement No 856688, European Forum on Paradox and Pluralism, which has supported our collaboration and enabled us to make this book Open Access.

We thank our colleagues Dr. Mustafa Kavas, Dr. Eli Krull, Dr. Katie Meissner, and Dr. Corinne Unger, who helped us manage and code this mass and very diverse dataset over several years, remaining good-humored and constructive throughout. Special thanks are due to our research assistant Rhianna Gallagher Rodgers, who supported us in the final year of pulling the analyses together and finalizing this book. You are all invaluable teammates.

Thank you to Associate Professor Rebecca Elliott, Professor Liz McFall, Dr. Ramona Meyricke, Dr. Zac Taylor, and Professor Andreas Tsanakas for their constructive comments on draft chapters, as well as to the many universities and colleagues who let us present drafts of different chapters over time. We are also indebted to Graham Topping for his feedback, critical eye, and for playing such an important role in pushing us to clarify our concepts.

Finally, we each have personal thanks. I (Paula) thank Huguette Haag and Poppy, who gave me a peaceful space, great snacks, and loving canine company as I wrote during the pandemic. I also thank my husband, Nick Rice, who remained encouraging throughout the whole long process.

I (Konstantinos) would like to thank my family, my mother (Dora), my father (Makis), and my brother (Alex), for all the unconditional support throughout my life and for helping me get here. I am also thankful to my partner (Karolina) who was supportive of me and tolerant of my mood swings while writing and rewriting this book.

I (Eugenia) wish to thank Stefano, without whom this (and so much else) would not have been possible; and Enrico, Pietro, and Teresa for graciously putting up with many an insurance-based dinner conversation.

I (Rebecca) would like to thank my little family. My children were born while collecting data for (Harrison) and then while writing (Grace) this book. Thank you, James, for juggling work and family alongside me and making it all possible.

We emphasize that the views expressed in this book are our own and do not reflect any authorization or endorsement by those we mention here. Additionally, while much that is good in the book is due to their help, any errors or oversights remain our own.

1

Protection Gap Entities

Saving insurance from itself?

Introductory Case

New Zealand (NZ) Earthquake Commission: Making disaster insurance widespread. NZ is one of the most risk-exposed countries in the world, and also among the most insured against disasters. During the 2010–11 Christchurch earthquakes, four major earthquakes and over 11,200 after-shocks shook the city. The most devastating, in February 2011, killed 185 people and forever changed the city center. At the time, almost 90 percent of NZ homeowners were insured for earthquake.[1] This meant that the disaster, in a small corner of the world with a city of under 400,000 people, was the most heavily insured seismological disaster in history[2] and the fourth most costly insurance event the world had ever seen. As Swiss Re, a large global reinsurer, asked: "could a small aftershock in a city not considered an earthquake hotspot trigger one of the largest losses ever?" Christchurch provided an emphatic "Yes!"[3]

In NZ, the fact that high-risk of earthquake is coupled with high levels of disaster insurance is partly explained through the existence of the New Zealand Earthquake Commission (EQC).[4] The precursor to this entity was established in the 1940s as a public insurance mechanism to address the gap between the risk of disaster from earthquake and insurance cover. There is a growing number of such entities across the world, set up to tackle various local insurance "protection gaps": for this reason, we call them Protection Gap Entities (PGEs). The aftermath of the Christchurch earthquakes would have been potentially very different without the EQC, which ensured that most people had insurance to help recover and rebuild.

EQC (initially named the "Earthquake and War Damage Commission") was established following earthquakes in the 1920–30s. As a Minister noted in parliament at the time: "most of the private insurance companies refuse—anyhow, here in Wellington [the capital of NZ, which sits on an earthquake faultline]—to take any further cover against earthquake risk."[5]

Disaster Insurance Reimagined. Paula Jarzabkowski et al., Oxford University Press. © Paula Jarzabkowski, Konstantinos Chalkias, Eugenia Cacciatori, and Rebecca Bednarek (2023). DOI: 10.1093/oso/9780192865168.003.0001

Properties in Wellington and other known earthquake-prone areas were considered so high-risk by private insurers that they could not insure them profitably. This meant that people "who wanted to insure themselves had no opportunity of doing so."[6] Even if a homeowner could find insurance, it was typically so expensive that it was out of reach for most. Recognizing this, the government of the day founded a PGE. Through a compulsory levy on all fire insurance policies, the new PGE would provide affordable earthquake insurance, ultimately for residential properties.

In 2010, when Christchurch began to shake, residential property owners in the entire country were paying the same government levy to EQC, regardless of whether they lived in an earthquake-exposed area. In any individual policy, this levy covered the first NZ$100k (~US $70k) of any earthquake damage. Private insurers then set their price for the rest of the policy (including for damages above that $100k). By covering the initial portion of the policy, which was the most likely to occasion claims after an earthquake, the EQC kept earthquake insurance affordable.

The 2010–11 Christchurch earthquakes resulted in more than 460,000 EQC claims being made. Drawing on the national disaster fund EQC had accumulated via the levies, as well as the reinsurance they had purchased, EQC was able to pay a total of NZ$10 billion (~US $7.7 billion) on these claims without drawing on additional government funding. Private insurers also paid NZ$21 billion (~US $16.1 billion).[7] As the total economic cost was estimated at NZ$40 billion (~US $30.8 billion), the combination of PGE cover, alongside private sector cover, very significantly reduced the burden of the loss and facilitated the recovery. By comparison, if a similar-sized disaster had hit other earthquake-prone regions such as Japan and California, it is estimated that their homeowners would have received just US $1.6 billion and US $0.7 billion respectively. In Japan, for example, Swiss Re estimates that the share of overall earthquake losses compensated for would be around 15 percent[8]—far short of the 77 percent of Christchurch losses covered.

This example demonstrates that PGEs can make a positive, large, and indeed crucial difference in recovery from disaster. Yet these entities are also always complex and surrounded by debate. The complexity and delays in settling claims through a public-private mechanism led people to question the EQC. Spurred by debate and dissatisfaction over "the Commission's operational practices and the Commission's approaches to claims outcomes in relation to the Christchurch earthquake events" a Public Inquiry into EQC ensued.[9] The inquiry incorporated different stakeholder views into recommendations to improve both pre-disaster readiness and post-disaster response.

1.1 Introduction

As this example of the Christchurch earthquakes shows, insurance is a key part of post-disaster recovery. A highly insured country like NZ has the financial capacity to rebuild after even a major disaster. However, as the NZ government noticed in the 1940s, being highly insured cannot be taken for granted. Hence, Protection Gap Entities (PGEs), like the EQC, are formed to ensure disaster insurance remains available. This book examines the growing role and importance of PGEs in providing disaster insurance around the world.

Private-sector disaster insurance works best at a sweet spot amongst three sets of tensions over who is in control of the insurance market (the control paradox), how much is known about the risk to be insured (the knowledge paradox), and who is responsible for paying for protection (the responsibility paradox). Due to the climate crisis and other geopolitical risk factors, these paradoxes are increasingly imbalanced, leading to a breakdown in private-sector disaster insurance in many parts of the world. Our book explains, with practical examples from different countries, how PGEs step in to maintain disaster insurance when these paradoxes become imbalanced. Drawing from our research into 17 PGEs operating across 49 countries over five years,[10] we examine strengths, limitations, and evolution of PGEs in providing disaster protection in the face of a growing insurance crisis. We conclude by reimagining disaster insurance as a key tool in an ecosystem that has societal protection from disaster at its heart.

This book is aimed at informed practitioners and policymakers who want to know more about how to protect homes, businesses, and society from disaster. We aim to make the complex topic of disaster insurance accessible and clear, to help support a transformation toward greater disaster protection.

1.2 Disasters are often uninsurable, leaving people unprotected

Disasters, such as earthquakes, hurricanes, floods, terrorist attacks, and pandemics, are ubiquitous in the global human experience. They devastate lives and livelihoods. Recovering from the losses and reconstructing after disasters is a costly business, often with long-term economic and social consequences. For instance, small, low-income countries can lose over 200 percent of their GDP from a single disaster, as happened in 2017 to Caribbean islands such as the Dominican Republic, following Hurricane Maria.[11] As one participant in our research explained, the after-effects of disasters can escalate rapidly: "there was an implosion of public services and public institutions after the hurricane and the people started looting and they had to bring in the military . . . to re-establish order" (Interview—Insurance Industry). Even wealthy countries suffer losses that devastate the livelihoods of individuals and communities. For example, the USA Federal Emergency Management Agency reports that 25 percent of US small businesses do not reopen after an extreme weather disaster.[12] The inability to recover from disasters is one key source of inequality and long-term poverty, both within and across countries.[13]

Disaster insurance is one important source of the financial resources needed to reduce the short- and long-term economic and social costs of disasters. Disaster insurance (sometimes called catastrophe insurance) refers to insurance of relatively low-frequency disasters with the potential for above-average or severe losses.[14] The amount of loss considered catastrophic varies between countries. However, such events are typically considered disastrous because, like the Christchurch earthquakes, they impact multiple policies simultaneously. These events include so-called "natural disasters," meaning extreme weather and seismological events,[15] as well as cyber-attacks, infectious diseases, and terrorist attacks.[16] In this book, we use the term disaster insurance to refer to all insurance for such disasters.

When a country is highly insured, capital from the global (re)insurance industry pays much of the cost of recovery, relieving government and private citizens of a large part of the financial burden. Insurance protection works through a process of risk transfer, explained in Appendix A. Briefly, property owners transfer the risk of a loss to an insurer, in exchange for a premium. The insurer agrees to pay for losses to any particular policyholder and, in exchange, makes a profit from the difference between the total premiums received and the total losses paid. The insurer then transfers some of the risk of a disaster, which will generate losses to many policyholders at once, to a reinsurer in exchange for premium. The reinsurer, in turn, makes a profit from the difference between premiums received from and the claims paid on the combined losses of insurers.

Importantly, insurance is a form of anticipatory financing,[17] which means that the flow of capital for recovery has been put in place before the disaster. Thus, insurance avoids the mad scramble to find cash immediately after a disaster. Insurance also dampens the effects of disasters by providing certainty that there will be money to pay for the clean-up and rebuilding of homes and communities.[18] Indeed, in the case of the Christchurch earthquake economic recovery was ultimately facilitated by the high levels of insurance generated by the EQC.[19]

When insurance coverage is low, the post-disaster injection of cash needed to finance response and recovery can be provided by some combination of private financial resources of individual citizens, government support, and charity and donor funding. There are important limitations to drawing on these resources. Many citizens do not have the financial resources to absorb the losses, and charity and donor funding are typically insufficient and slow.[20] In wealthy countries, this makes the government the provider of ultimate support. However, governments increasingly face budget constraints, so the amount and speed of fund delivery can be lower than public perception. Financing disaster-response and recovery can create large debts—as shown by the COVID-19 crisis—and divert public spending from other critical services such as healthcare, education, and infrastructure in ways that affect both current and future generations. In lower-income countries, the government may simply not have the resources to respond, generating an escalating spiral of effects that can set a country back decades. As one participant explained: "donors come to the rescue, but it takes quite a while. It takes three, six months, one year. And then you start renegotiating your debt schedule, and that also takes six months to a year, and in the meantime, you're in default and . . . [trails off]" (Interview—Development Agency). The very real risk is that much of the money needed to finance recovery will not be available, or will arrive too late, resulting in long-term issues in the disaster-zone such as reduction in growth, income, and education funding.[21] Insurance is thus a critical element in societal protection from the impact of disasters.[22]

There is increasing concern that the total losses from disasters are growing faster than the proportion of insured losses. The portion of uninsured losses is known as the "insurance Protection Gap."[23] In 2020 alone some 76 percent of losses from extreme weather or seismological disasters were uninsured, equating to US $231 billion.[24] The burden of paying for those uninsured losses fell upon governments, businesses, and individuals; in many cases losses were simply not compensated, leaving people and their communities with little capability to recover.

There are many reasons for these insurance protection gaps. Some derive from the consumer side. People struggle to calculate the benefits of insurance for protection from low-frequency, high-loss disasters[25] or expect that the government will intervene with special funding after a disaster.[26] Others relate to the supply side, when insurance is unavailable (as was the case for earthquake in NZ prior to the 1940s establishment of the EQC) or prohibitively expensive (as in flood-prone areas of many countries today).

We term this latter type of risk "uninsurable" because private-sector insurance is either unavailable or so highly priced that it is unaffordable to those at risk of disaster.[27] The protection gap refers to all uninsured economic loss, including assets for which insurance is available and affordable but which has not been purchased by consumers. By contrast, our particular concern is with risk that is *uninsurable* in practice, meaning that private-sector insurance is either unavailable or unaffordable.

There are three main reasons why risk is, or becomes, uninsurable based on this definition (see Chapter 2 for PGEs' origination):

1. **Frequency of loss.** Insurers are reluctant to offer policies on properties that are prone to frequent losses, such as those that flood regularly. If policies are available, the high premiums required typically make insurance unaffordable for people in these areas.

2. **Surprising and severe loss.** When the severity of a loss is surprising insurers often withdraw from offering policies for that specific disaster. This is what happened with the unexpected US $35 billion insurance loss[28] from the 2001 attack on the World Trade Center. The magnitude of the loss was a shock as previous terrorist attacks had never incurred more than a US $1 billion loss.[29] As a result, (re)insurers suddenly stopped offering terrorism insurance policies, making terrorism insurance unavailable.

3. **Insufficient revenue to stimulate a private insurance sector.** Offering insurance requires investment in risk-modeling, pricing, products, and administrative infrastructure. In low-income countries where there is likely to be low demand for insurance products,[30] there is little economic incentive for the development of a private insurance sector. While such countries may need disaster protection, insurance as a purely private-sector product would, therefore, simply be unavailable or unaffordable.

1.3 Protection Gap Entities as one solution to uninsurability

When disaster risk is uninsurable governments can decide to form what we have termed a "Protection Gap Entity" (PGE).[31] A PGE is a not-for-profit insurance scheme that is brought about through government legislation, in collaboration with the insurance industry and other stakeholders, to enable insurance protection for some specific type of disaster in a country. For example, the NZ government established the EQC to cover earthquake risk, and the USA put in place the Terrorism Risk Insurance Act (TRIA) for terrorism risk following the 2001 World Trade Centre attacks. Each of these is a form of PGE that enables insurance provision under some mix of government and insurance industry interaction.[32]

Broadly, PGEs adopt the following two strategies—either alone or in combination—to restore insurance in the face of uninsurable disasters[33] (see Appendix A for further explanation of how PGEs intervene in the risk-transfer process):

1. **Risk removal** moves some or all of the disaster risk from the insurance industry onto the balance sheet of the PGE (and potentially then transfers some of it to the government). Risk removal is particularly likely for risk that is seen as too volatile or extreme for the industry to take, such as terrorism. Insurance companies may still issue policies for disaster risk and accept premiums in return, but then pass some or most of the premium on to the PGE depending on the amount of risk the PGE takes on. The PGE can cover the exceptional risk of loss because, in addition to reinsurance capital, it has access to a government guarantee of funds. For example, the Australian Reinsurance Pool Corporation (ARPC) provides cover for terrorism risk in Australia. Losses above $200 million AUD (US $128 million) will be paid through the ARPC's own pool of premiums, followed by the reinsurance it has bought, and the remainder, up to $10 billion AUD (US $6.4 billion) will be paid by the government. The government guarantee means that the potential for very high losses from a terrorist disaster can be paid.
2. **Risk redistribution** takes the risk of loss by a relatively small group of high-risk policyholders and shares it across the wider pool of policyholders through a subsidy. These lower-risk policyholders pay a levy—a slightly higher premium than they would normally have to—and this levy is used to subsidize affordable premiums for those at high-risk. The PGE receives the premiums from all policyholders and uses the levy to smooth pricing across all insured policyholders. For example, Flood Re in the UK receives a levy from properties at low risk of flood, which it uses to subsidize policies for those at high-risk, so offering them affordable flood insurance. Other approaches, such as the KGVs (Cantonal Building Insurance companies) in Switzerland, make insurance mandatory across a population so that it can be offered at a fixed, affordable price to all policyholders.

PGEs provide significant economic and related social benefits in both developed and developing economies. For example, in Spain, the PGE, Consorcio de Compensación de Seguros (Consorcio), paid 92,485 claims for a total value of around €528 million (~US $516) in 2021.[34] In the aftermath of 9/11, the formation of TRIA in the USA allowed the continuation of large construction projects that had halted due to a lack of terrorism protection. In low- and middle-income Caribbean, African, and Pacific countries, PGEs made 78 disaster insurance payments between 2008 and 2020, providing cash flow for rapid responses to disasters such as hurricanes, earthquakes, and droughts.

As problems of uninsurability grow governments are increasingly looking to PGEs to take on new areas of uninsurable risk. For example, the California Earthquake Authority (CEA), established to provide earthquake insurance in 1996, was appointed as administrator of the California Wildfire Fund in 2020 to address problems in insuring wildfires.[35] In July 2022 the ARPC, which covers terrorism reinsurance in Australia, also took responsibility for a new cyclone reinsurance pool.[36]

While they can be effective at enabling insurance and are increasing in prevalence, PGEs are also often criticized. As illustrated by the "Public Inquiry into the Earthquake Commission" (NZ), PGEs especially face criticism after a disaster because disasters reveal the many complex and changing problems involved in insuring risk. For example, as shown by repeated flooding in part of the USA and Australia in recent years, some areas that are damaged cannot be recovered and some of these losses may not have been included in the remit of the PGE. PGEs need to evolve to meet these challenges, which place greater demands upon them, but also offer opportunities to expand their capacity to provide disaster protection.

This book examines the work of PGEs in addressing uninsurable risk, their limitations, and their potential as a wider solution for protection from disasters. But first, let's take a step back to look at how disaster insurance works and why it is breaking down.

1.4 The paradoxes at the heart of insurance

The boundary between insurability and uninsurability is often narrow: one disaster may tip a risk into uninsurability. For instance, earthquake risk in California following the 1994 Northridge earthquake, and terrorism risk in the UK following the 1992 IRA bombings of the Baltic Exchange.

To understand why some disaster risk becomes uninsurable, it is first necessary to understand how it is *made insurable* in the first place. Insurance is not simply a function of an innate or objective property of the risk in question. Rather, insurance is based upon finely balanced adjustments between a set of paradoxical forces—meaning forces that are contradictory but interdependent.[37] These paradoxes address three fundamental questions that are at the heart of insurance:

1. Who controls how the insurance market provides protection to society? In what we term the *control paradox*, the way that the market provides insurance protection necessitates some balance of control between the private insurance industry and the government.
2. How well is the risk understood? In what we term the *knowledge paradox*, risk must sit within the realm of sufficient knowledge—between too little knowledge and too much knowledge of the risk to be insured.
3. Who takes responsibility to pay for protection? In what we term the *responsibility paradox*, insured risk sits between the need for each individual to take responsibility for their own protection, and pay their premiums accordingly, and collective responsibility to cover each other's losses from the entire pool of premiums.

Risk is insurable when it is at the "sweet spot" of dynamic equilibrium, meaning continuous balancing within and between these three paradoxes (see Figure 1.1). Any ongoing imbalance between them might push some disaster risk out of the insurability zone. Let's now delve into these paradoxes.

1.4.1 The control paradox: Between industry and government

Insurance transfers the risk of a loss from a policyholder to an insurer and then a reinsurer in return for a premium (see Appendix A). This is a market activity because the risk of loss is treated as a commodity that can be exchanged for a price—a premium—between policyholder and insurer, with the insurer earning a profit. This ability to trade risks on a market is fundamental to the modern meaning of insurable risk.[38] While insurance is a market, control over who runs this market, how, and for whose benefit, sits between the private insurance industry and the government.

From an industry control perspective, it is relatively simple. Disaster risk is exchanged within a market, with the insurance industry making a profit in return for the service it offers; protection against loss. From a government control perspective, disaster risk is transferred in a market as a way to achieve some level of societal protection, in a process that is termed marketization.[39] Marketization occurs when activities that are important for society as a whole, such as education, healthcare, or protection from disaster, are

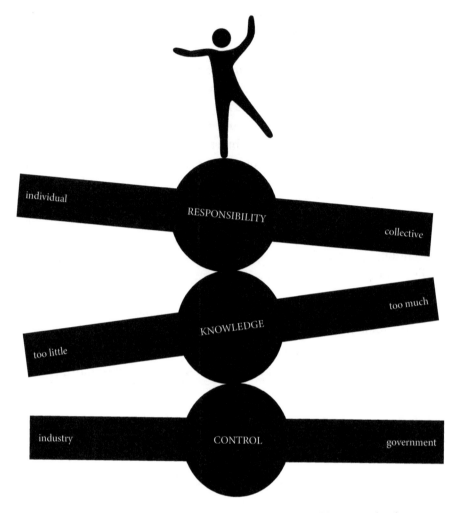

Figure 1.1 Viable insurance: Dynamic equilibrium within and between the three paradoxes of insurability.

provided through a market. Market processes are seen as an appropriate instrument to provide such goods because markets are considered to stimulate competition, innovation, incentives, economic value, and efficient use of resources.[40] The insurance market is seen by governments as an appropriate tool to provide financial protection from disaster because it already provides a critical safety net for many other important economic functions.[41] Insurance underpins economic activities that we take for granted and that could not take place or would be greatly reduced in its absence, from homeowner mortgages (through property insurance), to the movement of goods (through trade-credit insurance), to live entertainment (through live-event insurance), to owning and driving a car (through injury liability insurance). Often essential services, such as healthcare, are underpinned by private insurance, particularly in countries like the USA.[42] By providing this critical safety net the insurance market is a cornerstone of many activities that governments want or need to provide to their constituents. When that market is controlled by the private sector, we could even say that the protection function of insurance is outsourced from governments to the private sector.

Such use of the private sector—with its profit imperatives—to provide for social goals is a source of contradiction, even as the interdependence between social goals and profit imperatives is acknowledged.[43] In insurance markets, these tensions between profit and social objectives play out as a *paradox of control* between the insurance industry and the government. Even when protection is largely outsourced to industry, the government exercises control over the market through regulation to ensure transparency,[44] competitiveness,[45] and solvency to pay claims in the event of a disaster. At its most basic level, government control in the form of regulation aims to ensure that markets function as they should and deliver their efficiency and innovation benefits for society, rather than simply turning a profit for the insurance industry. However, the government might extend its control of markets when it deems that the social protection net provided, even by technically well-functioning markets, does not meet society's expectations of protection. These extensions of government control over the market are typically controversial. However, the government can never fully negate control of the insurance market, because it is the de facto "insurer of last resort."[46] If the disaster insurance market fails to provide a level of financial protection that society finds appropriate, the government must step in to pick up the pieces, paying for recovery through reallocating budgets and/or by borrowing. The two—insurance industry and government—are thus in a deeply interdependent, if also contested, relationship of control over the market that provides insurance-based financial protection to society.

The control paradox exists because the profit-oriented objectives of the industry do not always align with the wider social objectives of the government. However, for risk to be insurable, a balance must be maintained between a profitable insurance industry and sufficient government control to ensure that the industry provides a socially acceptable level of protection.[47] When this paradox becomes imbalanced for disaster insurance, governments often intervene in markets to protect citizens.[48] For example, in our opening vignette, the NZ government intervened to establish a market for a disaster (earthquake) that would not otherwise exist because the private insurance industry was refusing to provide that specific product.

1.4.2 The knowledge paradox: Between too much and too little knowledge

Whether a risk is insurable or not partly depends on whether insurers feel confident that they can calculate a price for it. Namely, a premium that will allow them to turn a profit once the losses of any individuals within a portfolio of risks have been paid.

Sufficient knowledge about a specific risk to carry out these calculations is thus an important factor in insurability.[49] Statistical knowledge enables disasters that cannot be individually predicted to be combined into a whole that can be predicted, and thus priced, with a reasonable level of certainty. An insurer does not know which individual policyholders will have their cars stolen this year, but via actuarial science, it does know with a reasonable level of confidence what the combined value of cars stolen from its pool of policyholders will be this year. This knowledge allows the price of insurance to be calculated. Conversely, uninsurability ensues when uncertainty is so high that statistics become useless in estimating the combined level of losses. Events such as the 1992 IRA London bombings and the 2001 World Trade Center attack generated uninsurability because they called into question the insurance industry's ability to calculate losses with a reasonable level of confidence.

Yet the relationship between insurability and knowledge is neither simple nor linear.[50] Excessive knowledge can also be damaging for insurability. For instance, when changes in climate mean that a property is certain to flood regularly, insurance for that property becomes unviable. If insurance is offered at all, the premium would need to cover almost the entirety of the loss to be economically viable for the insurer. A premium as costly as the loss itself makes insurance not only unaffordable but useless. Thus, there is no insurance market for risks that approximate certainties; it is essential for insurability in a private market that there remains an element of not knowing exactly what will occur and who will suffer which amount of loss in a given time frame.

Balancing the need to know enough but not too much about the risk of loss generates tensions over insurability. Recent advances in scientific understanding of weather and seismological phenomena, coupled with the increased availability of computer power, have improved knowledge about the potential combined losses for many disasters.[51] Such knowledge helps to expand the realm of insurability. However, sometimes the increase in knowledge means that it also becomes easy to calculate which exact property owner or building will be subjected to what level of losses, which is increasingly the case for floods.[52] As one PGE participant explained: "insurers [used to] cross-subsidize people at highest risk out of ignorance because they didn't know how to do it any better, and actually now we can differentiate flood risk at very high resolution" (Interview—Insurance Industry). Such advances in modeling lead to risk-reflective pricing, meaning a price that accurately reflects the potential for loss from individual policyholders. Risk-reflective pricing can, however, mean that the risk of loss on some properties can be pinpointed to the extent that they become uninsurable.

The knowledge paradox shows that knowledge is a blessing and a curse to insurance. A blessing because knowing the potential combined loss and ensuring that those individuals at most risk of loss can be appropriately charged enables risk to be transferred for a price. A curse because it reduces the domain of insurability by reducing the randomness of the loss of individuals. A degree of not knowing thus remains important. Balance is required between the extremes of too little and too much knowledge.

1.4.3 The responsibility paradox: Between individual and collective responsibility to pay

Insurance is based on the old adage that "the premiums of the many pay for the losses of the few." Individual policyholders pay a premium to transfer their individual risk to the insurance industry. Insurers pool these premiums and their associated risks and, because not all the policyholders will experience a loss, the payment for the losses of the few can be financed by the premiums of the many. Each individual buying insurance thus pays in advance for a fraction of the losses of other individuals in the collective, in exchange for their own risk of loss being covered.

Over centuries, insurance has built up around this collective principle that enables mutualization of individual risk.[53] Yet, individual and collective interests are always in tension and must be balanced for insurance to be possible.[54] Individuals need to bear fair responsibility for their risk to the collective,[55] and the pool needs to comprise enough individuals to compensate for the random misfortunes that might befall any of them.

Requiring individuals to bear fair responsibility for their risk has two distinct components. First, the system should avoid what is termed "moral hazard." This means that individuals, once insured, must not take excessive risk knowing that the cost of that risk will be borne by the collective rather than themselves. Examples of moral hazard include not locking a house or leaving high-value items beside an open window because insurance (via the premiums of the collective) will pay for any theft (again and again and again). Insurance contracts typically exclude losses arising from such behavior—for example, excluding theft arising from failure to secure property—thus disincentivizing moral hazard. Second, when individuals in a pool do not have the same potential risk of loss, premiums can be differentiated through risk-reflective pricing. For example, because recently licensed drivers are considered at more risk of accident, they are typically charged a high premium than those with longer, claims-free driving experience. This allows for a corrective to moral hazard. In disaster insurance higher-risk individuals, who, for instance, build on a beautiful but flood-exposed riverbank, may be required to pay more to compensate for their greater share of the risk to the collective.

A sufficiently large pool is a key condition for balancing individual and collective interests. Any individual must feel that the price to them is appropriate to their specific risk, and this price must also be sufficiently attractive that they will remain in the pool, so ensuring a large enough collective. Risk-reflective pricing generates tensions here. On the one hand, reducing the price for those at low risk means that they do not feel they are paying too high a premium and leave the pool. For example, those on hilltops would pay a lower premium for flood insurance than those who live at the seafront. On the other hand, fully risk-reflective pricing might mean that those at the seafront end up with an unaffordable premium and so leave the pool. When pricing does not meet the needs of either those at low or at high-risk, the overall size of the pool is reduced. It is, therefore, critical to insurability that risk-reflective pricing for individuals, ensuring their equal or "fair" participation in the collective, is balanced against ensuring a sufficiently large collective of insureds to spread that risk and reduce the cost for all.

1.5 Dynamic equilibrium and insurance

Insurability requires a dynamic equilibrium, meaning balance within and among the three paradoxes:[56] the control paradox, the knowledge paradox, and the responsibility paradox. As these paradoxes are connected, imbalance in one can escalate imbalance in another.[57] For instance, a major element of connection is the use of risk-reflective pricing arising from advances in knowledge about risk. Risk-reflective pricing influences the balance between individual and collective responsibility for loss, as individuals identifiable as high-risk may find their insurance unaffordable and drop out of the collective pool. This might in turn lead to imbalances in the control paradox, as society's desire for these individuals to be protected is no longer met by the insurance industry.

Insurability thus involves a highly dynamic equilibrium within and among these three paradoxes. Rather than a stable equal balance between poles, insurers can adjust any particular paradox in order to maintain balance among them to secure insurability.[58] For example, if insurers have a profitably diversified portfolio of risks, they can use their profitability to offset some of the price to high-risk individuals, so compensating for moderate imbalance in the knowledge and the responsibility paradoxes. When equilibrium is dynamically maintained, disaster risk remains insurable within the insurance industry. However, given the complexity and volatility of disasters, their insurability is always fragile. As disasters become more frequent or severe, or as our understanding of them changes, the system can tip over into disequilibrium. At this stage, PGEs may be established to address some of the consequent uninsurability.

1.6 Disequilibrium and the role of PGEs in building a new equilibrium

The dynamic equilibrium that defines insurability is under constant threat when it comes to disasters. Multiple factors from climate change, urbanization, global interdependence, and geopolitical instability, to changes in scientific knowledge about disaster risk are exerting increasing pressure on insurability.[59] Separately, any one of these factors has severe consequences for insurance as a global market. Taken together, they have compounding effects that amplify the potential for more frequent, severe, and concurrent losses.[60] When mass floods occur in multiple parts of the world simultaneously, with widespread wildfires in other regions, and hurricanes in yet another,[61] even as war and cyber-attacks threaten global supply chains, these losses are all paid from the same pool of global insurance capital at the same time. The global insurance market can absorb a certain number of severe losses within any year, but it cannot sustain severe losses from multiple disasters in multiple countries, concurrently, year-on-year.

These changes intensify imbalance within and between the three paradoxes that define insurability, as depicted in Figure 1.2. For example, the risks may become worse and/or more probable, such as changing weather patterns that

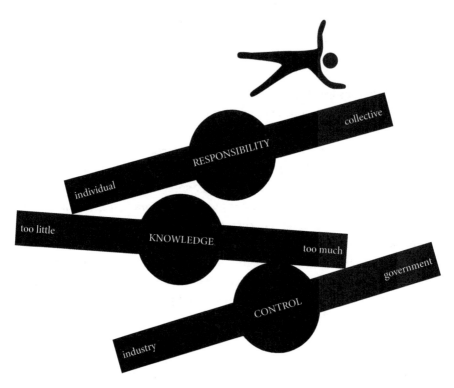

Figure 1.2 Imbalanced paradoxes generate disequilibrium in insurance.

make drought more widespread and severe. Risks may also become less pre-dictable or calculable, as illustrated by changing modes of terrorist attack, where it is difficult to predict what type of attack will take place, where, or how often. In these situations, the balance in the knowledge paradox changes in ways that have a knock-on effect on the other paradoxes.

Consider this scenario. As the number of properties at predictably high-risk increases, their risk-reflective premiums also rise, making insurance unaffordable for a growing number of homeowners. Other individuals face property losses so uncertain and volatile that their premiums cannot be calcu-lated, making insurance unavailable. Both types of individuals are, effectively, excluded from insurance, disrupting the balance between *individual* and *col-lective responsibility* to pay for protection. These imbalances arise because the insurance *industry* can no longer operate profitably on many disasters for many individuals, necessitating *government* intervention as the insur-ance market fails to provide societal protection. The compounding effect of these imbalanced paradoxes is disequilibrium, meaning that some disaster risks are no longer insurable in the private sector, even as the potential losses from these disasters escalate. The need for financial protection from disaster rises, even as the capability of the private insurance industry to provide that protection reduces. At this point, governments often turn to PGEs to "save insurance from itself."

Local instances of insurance disequilibrium have been felt for decades, where private-sector insurance could not be obtained at a sufficient level to meet that society's needs for protection. PGEs have arisen as within-country or within-region responses to such localized instances of disequilibrium. These PGEs include:

- single-risk schemes, such as the ARPC for Australian terrorism risk, or the UK Flood Re, intended to address the uninsurability of a specific disaster risk, such as terrorism, earthquake, or flood;
- multi-risk schemes, such as the Spanish Consorcio de Compensación de Seguros (Consorcio) or the French Caisse Centrale de Réassurance (CCR), intended to amalgamate a large enough collective pool of policyholders across several types of disaster that their collective premiums can be leveraged to protect society; and,
- multi-country schemes, such as the Caribbean Catastrophe Risk Insurance Facility (CCRIF) or the African Risk Capacity (ARC), intended to generate knowledge and develop insurance products that there would otherwise be no economic incentive to develop.

These PGEs have very different approaches to addressing the problem of uninsurable disaster risk, as the following examples illustrate. In Case 1.1, terrorism insurance in the USA, a PGE endeavors to rebuild industry control over the market, ensuring that the private sector for terrorism risk does not collapse while minimizing government intervention as much as possible. By contrast, in Case 1.2, disaster insurance in Spain, the government intervenes so comprehensively within the market that insurance through the PGE is a taken-for-granted feature of Spanish life.

Case example 1.1: TRIA: Minimizing government intervention in the market

TRIA was created in the aftermath of 9/11, when the insurance industry realized that it could not estimate combined losses for terrorism reliably. Hitherto unexpected modes of attack implied losses of such magnitude that the industry could not afford to hold sufficient capital in reserve to pay for them. The resultant withdrawal of insurance meant that businesses, reliant on insurance to trade, had to stop. For example, "construction projects just stalled" (Interview—Insurance Industry). TRIA was set up as a temporary three-year program to address this withdrawal of insurance.

The principles of TRIA are that losses above a certain threshold will be paid by the federal government in the immediate aftermath of a terrorist attack, after which the costs to the government will be recouped from the insurance industry by increasing the premiums to the entire insured population for a designated period. This promise of initial capital from the government to pay for immediate losses relieved the insurance industry of the burden to hold sufficient capital in reserve, enabling it to continue offering terrorism insurance. Since its inception, TRIA has been renewed four times. Each renewal involves the issue returning to Congress and much effort from industry bodies and insurers to argue that it is still needed (i.e., the uninsurability persists).

A vivid picture of renewing in 2015 was painted for us. The TRIA renewal should have been completed in 2014 but took until the following year. This meant TRIA briefly lapsed amongst the political kerfuffle. We could feel the stress and urgency in our discussions with participants even in 2016:

> The Chairman of the House of Financial Services Committee . . . just stopped everything to do with government programs . . . "private markets should solve their own problems" was his view. He just said "I don't agree" [with TRIA], and that was the end of the conversation. . . . that's why it lapsed, and then it lapsed again. (Interview—Insurance Industry)

Other stakeholders had to make strong arguments for the rationale behind TRIA and the ongoing involvement of the government in terrorism insurance. TRIA was ultimately renewed because it was still needed: "AM Best [a credit rating agency] did some analysis and pretty much said they had basically identified 40–50 insurance companies that they put on—essentially—a solvency watch list in the event that TRIA wasn't reauthorized" (Interview—Government). However, the ongoing temporary nature of the program reflects the fact that many stakeholders in the USA are extremely cautious about any government intervention in the market. They seek to keep the PGE to the absolute minimum; and "every few years it comes up for renewal . . . and it's just a disruption and a waste of time. Because at the end of the day it's something that's needed" (Interview—Insurance Industry).

The heated debates surrounding the TRIA renewal in the USA about whether the government should play any role in disaster insurance show how controversial PGEs often are. We found these controversies in many settings in our study, where participants would typically envision a circumscribed role for PGEs. The issue of how to limit "distortions" in the market was never far from the discussion. As one insurer claimed, "the very existence of [the PGE] crowds out the private sector" (Interview—PGE). Yet, as shown in Case 1.2, not all government intervention in markets is controversial. Rather, sometimes government control is welcomed as a valuable solution to disaster insurance.

Case example 1.2: Consorcio: Taken-for-granted government control over the market

Consorcio de Compensación de Seguros (Consorcio) is a government-owned insurer that sits alongside the private industry and provides almost all of Spain's disaster insurance. By applying a surcharge on property insurance premiums, it builds capital reserves to pay the disaster claims.[a] As private-sector insurers are usually highly resistant to such a broad government remit, when we began our interviews in Spain, we were expecting the usual strong opinions, or at least some unease or dissent. Instead, participants were almost universally supportive of Consorcio. An industry representative told us: "Consorcio is really a good institution. It's unique, I could say worldwide, and this is really special" (Interview—Insurance Industry). Another remarked: "I think that this system is good. It is well managed and is accepted with all the parts of the market and industry . . . and the premiums compensate for the losses" (Interview—Insurance Industry). It was not uncommon for questions about what to do to improve the system to be met with blank looks, and there seemed to be little appetite in the industry to take disaster risk on their own balance sheet.

As our research progressed, it became increasingly clear that there was very little debate or questioning of Consorcio. Part of this was due to Consorcio's broad, longstanding mandate for disaster cover. This cover is provided automatically to both individuals and businesses, within regular insurance policies and at a geographically flat rate that enables even those at high-risk to be insured. Because the cover is so comprehensive and has been in place for many decades, it provides the safety net needed to pay losses, meaning that there is minimal private disaster insurance activity in Spain. There is also little conflict over this government control of the market because of Consorcio's governance. Its board comprises six insurance industry representatives and six government representatives, so embedding interaction between industry needs to remain profitable and the government's need for comprehensive protection. It is also partly due to Consorcio's effectiveness in addressing the claims of Spanish citizens.

"In Spain natural hazards all belong to Consorcio. Basically, in Spain, we have a very different way of perceiving things. Everyone really pays very little to be insured, so the majority of people are insured. It's a system that's proven to be working, the earthquake of recent times has been almost all paid off thanks to Consorcio" (Interview—Government).

The overall effect is that Consorcio is usually considered effective and is well-regarded as an institution providing a useful service to the public and the insurance industry. Consorcio has made disaster insurance an infrastructure of Spanish society. Available to most without fuss, hardly thought about and questioned, in the same way that we do not think about electricity or running water in the normal course of things. The contrast with other PGEs, such as TRIA, is marked.

[a] Source: Consorcio de Compensación de Seguros, *An Overview*. Madrid: Consorcio de Compensación de Seguros, 2020. Available from: https://www.consorseguros.es/web/documents/10184/48069/CCS2016_EN.pdf/b7ed4f5e-6400-41f5-a1fb-d98e5f6a3778.

1.7 Saving insurance from itself?

PGEs expand the array of options involved in making disaster risk insurable. This means they can build a new equilibrium from which insurability ensues. Yet, as shown in the two case examples, the way that PGEs generate a new equilibrium varies dramatically. They do not all simply endeavor to restore a pre-existing balance within and among the three paradoxes—and indeed this may not be possible. Rather, PGEs create new forms of balance by fundamentally reshaping the paradoxes (see Chapter 3). Examples of how PGEs reshape the paradoxes include:

- The control paradox, by leveraging government capital alongside or at levels unavailable in the global insurance industry. This is shown in various terrorism PGEs such as the ARPC or TRIA, where government guarantees to pay for losses enable private sector insurance to operate.
- The knowledge paradox, by overlooking the detailed knowledge and associated pricing of those at high-risk to keep their premiums affordable and enable them to remain insured. This occurs in the Consorcio example (Case 1.2).

- The responsibility paradox, by moving the balance decisively toward collective responsibility to support high-risk individuals, as with Consorcio.

Such changes are fundamental and wide-reaching. They typically entail additional government control in the form of new legislation, the inclusion of new stakeholders, and the development of new knowledge about disasters. Hence, while different PGE initiatives can "save disaster insurance" by making otherwise uninsurable risk insurable in specific local contexts, their evolution is not smooth. They are typically fraught with contradictions as their different governments, insurance industry, and wider society stakeholders have different understandings of risk and protection and expect different things from them.[62] Furthermore, they may have unintended consequences that exacerbate disequilibrium. For example, the National Flood Insurance Program (NFIP) in the USA has been criticized for subsidizing insurance that enables at-risk individuals in the USA to keep rebuilding in high-risk areas.[63] In such examples, a PGE can exacerbate imbalances in the responsibility paradox by limiting the incentives of individuals to minimize their risk to the collective.

Nonetheless, despite these challenges, as disaster risk is becoming more uninsurable, the scope of PGEs is increasing. In this book, we examine how PGEs tackle disequilibrium to build disaster protection within their focal regions, and how their strategies for building new equilibria might combine to reconfigure global insurance markets. We propose ways that PGEs can further evolve to make the insurance system more sustainable within a climate-changed and more disaster-prone future. As the global insurance market is both the cornerstone of much economic and social activity, and also fragile in the face of the climate crisis and geopolitical change, such knowledge is vital to all our futures.

1.8 Book structure

This book builds from our research into 17 PGEs operating in 49 countries around the world over five years from 2016 to 2020 (see Appendix B). Drawing upon our deep immersion in the world of PGEs, we present the following chapters on the work of these important organizations.

Chapter 2, "Paradoxes of origination: Between too little and too much knowledge," is grounded in the knowledge paradox. We examine the origins of PGEs, explaining how they originate at points where there is either insufficient knowledge for risk to be insured in the private sector, or where knowledge is so precise that it excludes many people from the pool of poli-cyholders. We also show two main ways that PGEs intervene in the private market to counteract those knowledge problems.

Chapter 3, "Shouldering the burden: Who controls the market and has responsibility for protection?" is grounded in the links between the control and responsibility paradoxes. It lays out the variation between PGEs from those with an industry orientation, such as TRIA (Case example 1.1) to a government orientation like Consorcio (Case example 1.2). We show how different orientations toward industry or government control align with different assumptions about individual or collective responsibility for protection from loss. We also investigate the successes and challenges of designing PGEs in different ways and how this affects the wider question of uninsurability.

Chapter 4 is "Problem solved? Between static remits and evolving environments." A PGE is established with a remit that is partial. It solves some specific problem of uninsurable risk within a country at a moment in time. Yet the risk environment is constantly changing. PGEs must thus evolve to address emerging areas of uninsurable risk. Disasters are an important trigger for evolution because they expose risk that is not insured and highlight the urgency of a response. Yet, even after a disaster, as we explain, different orientations toward industry or government control over the insurance market make this evolution more contested or collaborative. And always complex.

Chapter 5 is "Limiting loss: Between financial and physical resilience." PGEs are set up to provide financial protection by making insurance available, but this is only one aspect of the problem. To increase the insurability of risk-exposed assets, such as houses on flood plains, it is also necessary to limit the losses by increasing the physical resilience of these assets. In this chapter we explain why some PGEs have evolved to play an active role in limiting loss in this way, while others struggle to balance these two aspects of increasing insurability.

Our concluding chapter, "Reimagining disaster insurance: Toward a new equilibrium," considers how the global insurance system can remain relevant in a world of increasingly catastrophic disasters. In the context of increasingly frequent, severe, and concurrent disasters, where private-sector insurance is failing, we expand upon the opportunities for PGEs, systematically developed and designed, to play a part in a reimagined insurance landscape. We offer a vision for how to reimagine insurance within the ecosystem of protection: embracing knowledge to build stronger links between physical and financial resilience; acknowledging government and industry collaboration in insurance markets; and accepting that collective responsibility for protection will be necessary to enable individuals to act responsibly in their own protection.

Each chapter hangs upon our core scaffold of how PGEs work to create new equilibrium within and between the three paradoxes that characterize the global insurance system—using a wider range of tools than the private insurance industry has when working alone. The work of these PGEs is difficult and complex. We aim to provide coherent and evocative insights to an informed public that is interested in the ongoing viability of insurance as a mechanism for protection from disaster.

Notes

1. National Emergency Management Agency, *2016 Earthquake Recovery: Residential Insurance*. Wellington: New Zealand Government. Date accessed: September 2022. Available from: https://www.civildefence.govt.nz/resources/november-2016-earthquake-recovery/housing/residential-insurance/
2. Nguyen, C. N., Noy, I., "Comparing Earthquake Insurance Programmes: How Would Japan and California have Fared after the 2010–11 Earthquakes in New Zealand?" *Disasters*, 44(2) (2020): 367–89. https://doi.org/10.1111/disa.12371
3. Grollimund, B., *Small Quakes, Big Impact: Lessons Learned from Christchurch*. Zurich: Swiss Re, 2014. Available from: https://www.swissre.com/dam/jcr:57469cc6-0a23-4100-8fe4-00663af35ad0/lessons_from_christchurch_web.pdf.

   Department of the Prime Minister and Cabinet, *Inquiry into the EQC*. Wellington: New Zealand Hovernment. Last updated December 13, 2021. Available from: https://eqcinquiry.govt.nz/assets/Inquiry-Reports/Report-of-the-Public-Inquiry-into-EQC.pdf
4. As of 2022 EQC is transitioning to its new name: "Toka Tū Ake—Natural Hazards Commission"—to "better reflect EQC's unique insurance scheme, the range of natural hazards it covers and EQC's expertise around those hazards" beyond earthquake; EQC, "Introducing EQC's future name: Toka Tū Ake—Natural Hazards Commission," EQC. March 23, 2022. Available from: https://www.eqc.govt.nz/news/introducing-eqcs-future-name-toka-tu-ake-natural-hazards-commission/
5. New Zealand, *Parliamentary Debates*, vol. 612, February 22, 1944, Arnold Nordmeyer. Date accessed: September 2022. Available from: https://hdl.handle.net/2027/uc1.32106019929824
6. New Zealand, *Parliamentary Debates*, February 22, 1944, Arnold Nordmeyer.
7. Insurance Council of New Zealand, *Canterbury Earthquakes*. Wellington: Insurance Council of New Zealand. Date accessed: September 2022. Available from: https://www.icnz.org.nz/natural-disasters/canterbury-earthquakes.

   Department of the Prime Minister and Cabinet, *Public Inquiry into the Earthquake Commission: Report of the Public Inquiry into the Earthquake Commission*. Wellington: New Zealand Government, March 2020. Available from: https://dpmc.govt.nz/sites/default/files/2021-01/report-of-the-public-inquiry-into-the-earthquake-commission.pdf
8. Nguyen, Noy, "Comparing Earthquake Insurance Programmes."

   Sheehan, M., "Japan's Earthquake Protection Gap Estimated at $25bn by Swiss Re." *Reinsurance News*, March 11, 2021. Available from: https://www.reinsurancene.ws/japans-earthquake-protection-gap-estimated-at-25bn-by-swiss-re/

9. Dept of the Prime Minister and Cabinet, *Public Inquiry*.

10. At the time of going to press, we had studied the following PGEs: African Risk Capacity (ARC) which provided insurance to Burkina Faso, Chad, Cote d'Ivoire, the Gambia, Madagascar, Malawi, Mali, Mauritania, Niger, Senegal, Sudan, Togo, Zambia, and Zimbabwe; Australian Reinsurance Pool Corporation (ARPC—Australia); California Earthquake Authority (CEA—USA); Caisse Centrale de Réassurance (CCR—France); Caribbean Catastrophe Risk Insurance Facility (CCRIF), which provided insurance to Anguilla, Antigua and Barbuda, the Bahamas, Barbados, Belize, Bermuda, British Virgin Islands, the Cayman Islands, Dominica, Grenada, Guatemala, Haiti, Jamaica, Montserrat, Nicaragua, Panama, Saint Kitts and Nevis, Saint Lucia, Sint Maarten, Saint Vincent and the Grenadines, the Republic of Trinidad and Tobago, the Turks and Caicos Islands; Consorcio de Compensación de Seguros—Spain; Earthquake Commission (EQC—NZ); Flood Re—UK; Fideicomiso Fondo de Desastres Naturales (FONDEN—Mexico); Gestion de l'Assurance et de la Réassurance des risques Attentats et actes de Terrorisme (GAREAT—France); National Flood Insurance Program (NFIP—USA); Pacific Catastrophe Risk Insurance Company (PCRIC), which provided insurance to Cook Islands, Samoa, Tonga; Pool Re—UK; Swiss system of Kantonale Gebäudeversicherungen (KGVs—Switzerland); South African Special Risk Association (SASRIA—South Africa); Turkish Catastrophe Insurance Pool (TCIP—Turkey); Terrorism Risk Insurance Act (TRIA—USA).

11. Government of the Commonwealth of Dominica, "Executive Summary: Post-Disaster Needs Assessment Hurricane Maria." Dominica: CARICOM, September 18, 2017. Available from: https://resilientcaribbean.caricom.org/wp-content/uploads/2017/11/DOMINICA-EXECUTIVE-SUMMARY.pdf

12. FEMA, "Stay in Business After a Disaster by Planning Ahead." Washington, DC: United States Government; release date October 30, 2018, last updated March 18, 2021. Available from: https://www.fema.gov/press-release/20210318/stay-business-after-disaster-planning-ahead

13. Clarke, D. J., Dercon, S., *Dull Disasters? How Planning Ahead will Make a Difference*. Oxford: Oxford University Press, 2016.

 Freudenburg, W. R., Gramling, R., Laska, S., Erikson, K. T., *Catastrophe in the Making: The Engineering of Katrina and the Disasters of Tomorrow*. Washington, DC: Island Press/Center for Resource Economics, 2012.

 Howell, J., Elliott, J. R., "Damages Done: The Longitudinal Impacts of Natural Hazards on Wealth Inequality in the United States." *Social Problems*, 66(3) (2019): 448–67. https://doi.org/10.1093/socpro/spy016

14. Lockett, J., "Catastrophes and Catastrophe Insurances." *Journal of the Staple Inn Actuarial Society*, 24 (1980): 91–134. https://doi.org/10.1017/S0020269X00009257

15. While the term natural catastrophe or natural disaster is typically used in insurance to refer to weather, geological, and seismological disasters, for many years it has been seen as a misnomer in development and environmental studies. This is because the triggers, such as tropical storms or droughts, may be natural phenomena but their catastrophic effects are exacerbated by human action, including both where and how land is used and climate change effects (see, e.g., Wijkman, A., Timberlake, L., *Natural Disasters: Acts of God or Acts of Man?* Abingdon, UK: Routledge; 2021.

16. OECD, *Enhancing Financial Protection against Catastrophe Risks: The Role of Catastrophe Risk Insurance Programmes*. Paris: OECD, October 11, 2021. Available from: www.oecd.org/daf/fin/insurance/Enhancing-financial-protection-against-catastrophe-risks.htm

17. Surminski, S., "Insurance Instruments for Climate-Resilient Development." In Fankhauser, S., McDermott, T. K. J., eds, *The Economics of Climate-Resilient Development*. Cheltenham, UK: Edward Elgar Publishing, 2016, chapter 10. <https://doi.org/10.4337/9781785360312.00020>.

18. Clarke, Dercon, *Dull Disasters?*.

19. Nguyen, C. N., Noy, I., "Measuring the Impact of Insurance on Urban Earthquake Recovery Using Nightlights." *Journal of Economic Geography*, 20(3) (2020): 857–77. https://doi.org/10.1093/jeg/lbz033

20. E.g.: Saez, P., Konyndyk, J., Worden, R., *Financing the Humanitarian Public Good: Towards a More Effective Humanitarian Financing Model*. Washington, DC: Center for Global Development, July 2021. Available from: https://www.cgdev.org/sites/default/files/More-effective-humanitarian-financing-model.pdf

21. Botzen, W. W., Deschenes, O., Sanders, M., "The Economic Impacts of Natural Disasters: A Review of Models and Empirical Studies." *Review of Environmental Economics and Policy*, 13(2) (2019): 167–88. https://doi.org/10.1093/reep/rez004.

    Noy, I., duPont IV, W., "The Long-Term Consequences of Disasters: What Do we Know, and What we Still Don't." *International Review of Environmental and Resource Economics*, 12(4) (2018): 325–54. <http://dx.doi.org/10.1561/101.00000104>.

22. Kousky, C., *Understanding Disaster Insurance: New Tools for a More Resilient Future*. Washington, DC: Island Press, 2022.

23. Schanz, K.-U., Wang, S., eds, *The Global Insurance Protection Gap: Assessment and Recommendations*. Geneva: Geneva Association, November 2014. Available from: https://www.genevaassociation.org/sites/default/files/research-topics-document-type/pdf_public/ga2014-the_global_insurance_protection_gap_1.pdf.

24. Swiss Re, *Resilience Index 2021: A Cyclical Growth Recovery, But Less Resilient World Economy*. Zurich: Sigma, Swiss Re Institute, June 2021. Available from: https://www.swissre.com/dam/jcr:ca784019-cd41-45fb-81ed-9379f2cd91e3/swiss-re-institute-sigma-resilience-index-update-june-2021.pdf

25. Kunreuther, H., Pauly, M., "Neglecting Disaster: Why Don't People Insure Against Large Losses?" *Journal of Risk and Uncertainty*, 28(1) (2004): 5–21. https://doi.org/10.1023/B:RISK.0000009433.25126.87

26. Raschky, P. A., Weck-Hannemann, H., "Charity Hazard—A Real Hazard to Natural Disaster Insurance?" *Environmental Hazards*, 7(4) (2007): 321–9. https://doi.org/10.1016/j.envhaz.2007.09.002

27. Hudson, P., Botzen, W. J. W., Feyen, L., Aerts, J. C. J. H., "Incentivising Flood Risk Adaptation through Risk Based Insurance Premiums: Trade-Offs between Affordability and Risk Reduction." *Ecological Economics*, 125 (2016): 1–3. <https://doi.org/10.1016/j.ecolecon.2016.01.015>.

28. European Central Bank, *Financial Stability Review December 2017*. Frankfurt: European Central Bank, November 29, 2017, 138–40: iii The Euro area financial system: Box 18, Terrorism insurance: Who insures and who is insured. Available from: https://www.ecb.europa.eu/pub/financial-stability/fsr/focus/2007/pdf/ecb~7585877f4b.fsrbox200712_18.pdf

29. Ericson, R., Doyle, A., "Catastrophe Risk, Insurance and Terrorism." *Economy and Society*, 33(2) (2004): 135–73. <https://doi.org/10.1080/03085140410001677102>.

30. Feyen, E., Lester, R. R., Rocha, R. D., "What Drives the Development of the Insurance Sector? An Empirical Analysis Based on a Panel of Developed and Developing Countries." *Journal of Financial Perspectives*, 1(1) (2013): 1–23. https://ssrn.com/abstract=3076016

31. Jarzabkowski, P., Chalkias, K., Cacciatori, E., Bednarek, R., *Between State and Market: Protection Gap Entities and Catastrophic Risk*. London: Cass Business School, City, University of London, June 26, 2018. Available from: https://www.bayes.city.ac.uk/__data/assets/pdf_file/0020/420257/PGE-Report-FINAL.pdf

32. Kunreuther, H., "The Role of Insurance in Reducing Losses from Extreme Events: The Need for Public-Private Partnerships." *The Geneva Papers on Risk and Insurance—Issues and Practice*, 40 (2015): 741–62. https://doi.org/10.1057/gpp.2015.14.

    McAneney, J., McAneney, D., Musulin, R., Walker, G., Crompton, R., "Government-Sponsored Natural Disaster Insurance Pools: A View from Down-Under." *International Journal of Disaster Risk Reduction*, 15 (2016): 1–9. https://doi.org/10.1016/j.ijdrr.2015.11.004.

    Bruggeman, V., Faure, M. G., Fiore, K., "The Government as Reinsurer of Catastrophe Risks?" *The Geneva Papers on Risk and Insurance-Issues and Practice*, 35(3) (2010): 369–90. https://doi.org/10.1057/gpp.2010.10.

    Kousky, C., *Understanding Disaster Insurance: New Tools for a More Resilient Future*. Washington, DC: Island Press, 2022.

33. Jarzabkowski et al., *Between State and Market*. Jarzabkowski, P., Krull, E., Kavas, M., Chalkias, K., "Strategies for Responding to Pandemic Risk: Removal and/or Redistribution." *Journal of Financial Transformation*, 54 (2021): 62–9. Available from: https://www.capco.com/Capco-Institute/Journal-54-Insurance/Strategies-For-Responding-To-Pandemic-Risk-Removal-And-Or-Redistribution

34. Consorcio de Compensación de Seguros, *Informe de la Actividad 2021*. Madrid: Consorcio de Compensación de Seguros, 2021. Available from: https://www.consorseguros.es/web/documents/10184/48069/INFORME_ACTIVIDAD_2016ESP.pdf/4c69bf69-6e30-4aac-944d-96c66a4516f7.

    Consorcio de Compensación de Seguros, *Estadistica riesgos extraordinarios 1971–2021*. Madrid: Consorcio de Compensación de Seguros, 2021. Available from: https://www.consorseguros.es/web/documents/10184/44193/Estadistica_Riesgos_Extraordinarios_1971_2014/14ca6778-2081-4060-a86d-728d9a17c522

35. California Wildfire Fund. Accessed September 2022. Available from: https://www.cawildfirefund.com

36. Australian Reinsurance Pool Corporation, *The Cyclone Pool*. Canberra: Australian Reinsurance Pool Corporation. Date accessed: September 2022. Available from: https://arpc.gov.au/what-we-do/the-cyclone-pool/

37. Bednarek, R., e Cunha, M. P., Schad, J., Smith W., "The Value of Interdisciplinary Research to Advance Paradox in Organization Theory." In Bednarek, R., e Cunha, M. P., Schad, J., Smith, W., eds, *Interdisciplinary Dialogues on Organizational Paradox: Learning from Belief and Science, Part A* (Research in the Sociology of Organizations, Vol. 73a). Bingley: Emerald Publishing, 2021, 3–25. https://doi.org/10.1108/S0733-558X2021000073a002.

Lewis, M. W., "Exploring Paradox: Toward a More Comprehensive Guide." *Academy of Management Review*, 25(4) (2000): 760–76. https://doi.org/10.5465/amr.2000.3707712.

Smith, W. K., Lewis, M. W., "Toward a Theory of Paradox: A Dynamic Equilibrium Model of Organizing." *Academy of Management Review*, 36(2) (2011): 381–403. https://doi.org/10.5465/amr.2009.0223.

Schad, J., Lewis, M. W., Raisch, S., Smith, W. K., "Paradox Research in Management Science: Looking Back to Move Forward." *Academy of Management Annals*, 10(1) (2016): 5–64. https://doi.org/10.5465/19416520.2016.1162422

38. Taylor, Z. J., Weinkle, J. L., "The Riskscapes of Re/insurance." *Cambridge Journal of Regions, Economy and Society*, 13(2) (2020): 405–22. https://doi.org/10.1093/cjres/rsaa015

39. Callon, M., "Revisiting Marketization: From Interface-Markets to Market-Agencements." *Consumption Markets and Culture*, 19(1) (2016): 17–37. https://doi.org/10.1080/10253866.2015.1067002.

Zelizer, V. A., *Morals and Markets: The Development of Life Insurance in the United States.* New York: Columbia University Press, 2017.

40. Davis, G. F., *Managed by the Markets: How Finance Re-Shaped America.* Oxford: Oxford University Press, 2009.

Ericson, R., Barry, D., Doyle, A., "The Moral Hazards of Neo-Liberalism: Lessons from the Private Insurance Industry." *Economy and Society*, 29(4) (2000): 532–58. https://doi.org/10.1080/03085140050174778.

Ferlie, E., Fitzgerald, L., Pettigrew, A., *The New Public Management in Action.* Oxford: Oxford University Press, 1996.

41. Hecht, S. B., "Climate Change and the Transformation of Risk: Insurance Matters." *UCLA Law Review*, 55(6) (2007): 1559–1620.

Grant, E., *The Social and Economic Value of Insurance.* Geneva: Geneva Association, September 2012. Available from https://www.genevaassociation.org/sites/default/files/research-topics-document-type/pdf_public//ga2012-the_social_and_economic_value_of_insurance.pdf

42. McFall, L., "Personalizing Solidarity? The Role of Self-Tracking in Health Insurance Pricing." *Economy and Society*, 48(1) (2019): 52–76. https://doi.org/10.1080/03085147.2019.1570707

43. Jarzabkowski, P., Bednarek, R., Chalkias, K., Cacciatori, E., "Enabling Rapid Financial Response to Disasters: Knotting and Reknotting Multiple Paradoxes in Interorganizational Systems." *Academy of Management Journal* (2021). https://doi.org/10.5465/amj.2019.0745.

Sharma, G., Bansal, P., "Partners for Good: How Business and NGOs Engage the Commercial–Social Paradox." *Organization Studies*, 38(3–4) (2017): 341–64. https://doi.org/10.1177/0170840616683739.

Smith, W. K., Besharov, M. L., "Bowing before Dual Gods: How Structured Flexibility Sustains Organizational Hybridity." *Administrative Science Quarterly*, 64(1) (2019): 1–44. https://doi.org/10.1177/0001839217750826

44. Skipper, H. D., Klein, R. W., "Insurance Regulation in the Public Interest: The Path towards Solvent, Competitive Markets." *The Geneva Papers on Risk and Insurance-Issues and Practice*, 25(4) (2000): 482–504. https://doi.org/10.1111/1468-0440.00078

45. Ericson, R. V., Doyle, A., Barry, D., Ericson, D., *Insurance as Governance*. Toronto: University of Toronto Press, 2003.

46. Baker, C., "The Federal Reserve as Last Resort." *University of Michigan Journal of Law Reform*, 46(1) (2012): 69–133. https://doi.org/10.36646/mjlr.46.1.federal

47. Hansen, M. B., Lindholst, A. C., "Marketization Revisited." *International Journal of Public Sector Management*, 29(5) (2016): 398–408. https://doi.org/10.1108/IJPSM-05-2016-0090

48. Elliott, R., *Underwater: Loss, Flood Insurance, and the Moral Economy of Climate Change in the United States*. New York: Columbia University Press, 2021.

49. Beck, U., "The Terrorist Threat: World Risk Society Revisited." *Theory, Culture and Society*, 19(4) (2002): 39–55. https://doi.org/10.1177/0263276402019004003

50. Collier, S. J., "Enacting Catastrophe: Preparedness, Insurance, Budgetary Rationalization." *Economy and Society*, 37(2) (2008): 224–50. https://doi.org/10.1080/03085140801933280.

    Taylor, Weinkle, "Riskscapes of Re/insurance."

51. Mitchell-Wallace, K., Jones, M., Hillier, J., Foote, M., *Natural Catastrophe Risk Management and Modelling: A Practitioner's Guide*. Hoboken, NJ: John Wiley & Sons, 2017.

52. Armal, S., Porter, J. R., Lingle, B., Chu, Z., Marston, M. L., Wing, O. E. J., "Assessing Property Level Economic Impacts of Climate in the US, New Insights and Evidence from a Comprehensive Flood Risk Assessment Tool." *Climate*, 8(10) (2020): 116. https://doi.org/10.3390/cli8100116

53. Borscheid, P., Gugerli, D., Straumann, T., *The Value of Risk: Swiss Re and the History of Reinsurance*. Oxford: Oxford University Press, 2013.

54. Baker, T., Simon, J., eds, *Embracing Risk: The Changing Culture of Insurance and Responsibility*. Chicago: University of Chicago Press, 2002.

55. Landes, X., "How Fair is Actuarial Fairness?" *Journal of Business Ethics*, 128(3) (2015): 519–33. https://doi.org/10.1007/s10551-014-2120-0.

    Lindholm, M., Richman, R., Tsanakas, A., Wuthrich, M. V., "A Discussion of Discrimination and Fairness in Insurance Pricing." *arXiv*, 2022. https://doi.org/10.48550/arXiv.2209.00858

56. Smith, W. K., Lewis, M. W., "Toward a Theory of Paradox: A Dynamic Equilibrium Model of Organizing." *Academy of Management Review*, 36(2) (2011): 381–403. https://doi.org/10.5465/amr.2009.0223

57. Jarzabkowski et al., "Enabling Rapid Financial Response to Disasters." Sheep, M.L., Fairhurst, G. T., Khazanchi, S., "Knots in the Discourse of Innovation: Investigating Multiple Tensions in a Reacquired Spin-Off." *Organization Studies*, 38(3–4) (2017): 463–88. https://doi.org/10.1177/0170840616640845

58. Weiser, A. K., Laamanen, T., "Extending the Dynamic Equilibrium Model of Paradox: Unveiling the Dissipative Dynamics in Organizations." *Organization Theory*, 3(3) (2022): 26317877221090317. https://doi.org/10.1177/26317877221090317

59. Boers, N., Goswami, B., Rheinwalt, A., Bookhagen, B., Hoskins, B., Kurths, J., "Complex Networks Reveal Global Pattern of Extreme-Rainfall Teleconnections." *Nature*, 566 (2019): 373–7. https://doi.org/10.1038/s41586-018-0872-x.

Collier, S. J., Elliott, R., Lehtonen, T. K., "Climate Change and Insurance." *Economy and Society*, 50(2) (2021): 158–72. https://doi.org/10.1080/03085147.2021.1903771.

Pörtner, H.-O., Roberts, D. C., Tignor, M., Poloczanska, E. S., Mintenbeck, K., Alegría, A., Craig, M., Langsdorf, S., Löschke, S., Möller, V., Okem, A., Rama, B., eds, *Climate Change 2022: Impacts, Adaptation and Vulnerability*. IPCC. Contribution of working group II to the sixth assessment report of the intergovernmental panel on climate change. Cambridge: Cambridge University Press, 2022. Available from https://www.ipcc.ch/report/ar6/wg2/downloads/report/IPCC_AR6_WGII_FullReport.pdf.

Ranger, N., Mahul, O., Monasterolo, I., "Managing the Financial Risks of Climate Change and Pandemics: What we Know (and Don't Know)." *One Earth*, 4(10) (2021): 1375–85. https://doi.org/10.1016/j.oneear.2021.09.017.

Taylor, Weinkle, "Riskscapes of Re/insurance."
60. Ranger et al., "Managing the Financial Risks."
61. Banholzer, S., Kossin, J., Donner, S., "The Impact of Climate Change on Natural Disasters." In Zommers, Z., Ashbindu, S., eds, *Reducing Disaster: Early Warning Systems for Climate Change*. Dordrecht: Springer, 2014, chapter 2. https://doi.org/10.1007/978-94-017-8598-3_2
62. Elliott, *Underwater*. Jarzabkowski, P., Bednarek, R., Chalkias, K., Cacciatori, E., "Exploring Inter-Organizational Paradoxes: Methodological Lessons from a Study of a Grand Challenge." *Strategic Organization*, 17(1) (2019): 120–32. https://doi.org/10.1177/1476127018805345
63. Elliott, Underwater. Bedient, P., quoted in Kimmelman, M., "Lessons from Hurricane Harvey: Houston's Struggle is America's Tale." *The New York Times*, November 11, 2017. Available from https://www.nytimes.com/interactive/2017/11/11/climate/houston-flooding-climate.html

2

Paradoxes of origination

Between too little and too much knowledge

2.1 Introduction

Protection Gap Entities (PGEs) are established when the uninsurability of some specific disaster becomes widely recognized as a societal crisis. Born out of government intervention, PGEs provide insurance for an otherwise uninsurable disaster, with purposes and in ways that are different from private insurers and reinsurers. In this chapter we explore what prompts the origination of PGEs, and how they enable some measure of disaster insurability to be established or re-established.

The knowledge paradox plays a central role in PGE origination. PGEs originate when the insurance system for one or more risks reaches a state of disequilibrium because of either too little or too much knowledge. We know too little to insure disasters when current knowledge is not enough to provide reliable estimates of losses; or when the perceived reliability of existing knowledge is suddenly challenged by unexpected disasters. We know too much when the steady accumulation of knowledge about a disaster allows ever-more-precise predictions of who will suffer specific losses. In either case disequilibrium can ensue in which disaster falls outside the zone of insurability.

In discussing these originating conditions, we also demonstrate the mechanisms through which PGEs can rebalance the knowledge paradox. For example, by ignoring too much knowledge that makes risk too predictable or by developing new knowledge to counteract the dearth of knowledge. Achieving a new balance in the knowledge paradox does not occur in isolation. It also necessitates shifts in the balancing between industry and government control over the insurance market and between individual and collective responsibility over who pays for disaster risk protection. We therefore touch upon how the establishment of PGEs to address the imbalance in the knowledge paradox produces a new balance in the control paradox. We also indicate how two primary market intervention strategies used

Disaster Insurance Reimagined. Paula Jarzabkowski et al., Oxford University Press. © Paula Jarzabkowski, Konstantinos Chalkias, Eugenia Cacciatori, and Rebecca Bednarek (2023). DOI: 10.1093/oso/9780192865168.003.0002

by PGEs, removal and redistribution of risk,[1] are instrumental in achieving a new balance in the responsibility paradoxes (see Chapter 3 for more detail). This interconnected rebalancing of the three paradoxes produces a new equilibrium in which insurance is possible.

2.2 At first, we did not know: The origination of early PGEs

Some PGEs date back to the first half of the twentieth century when disasters such as earthquakes or floods were still largely uninsured. In those days, the risk of loss associated with disasters was difficult to calculate in comparison to more recurrent and smaller disasters for which more data were available: "at the beginning, it was a challenge because even the insurer didn't want to insure these risks that were unknown, because there were no statistics, there was no technology for data collection" (Interview—PGE). Dealing with the outcomes of disasters was often left to goodwill, such as public charity, a situation that was seen in many places as increasingly problematic.

Switzerland provides a relevant example.[2] Floods were historically a key disaster in Switzerland and for a long time insurance for them was not available in the market. Significant societal discussion developed from the mid-nineteenth century onward around the need to offer protection, particularly to poor populations who could see their livelihood and several generations of accumulated savings in property destroyed by floods. During this period of economic growth and development, in which Switzerland was reshaping itself into a modern nation, the public fire insurance companies set up in the late eighteenth century were seen as a model that could be extended to other disasters such as flood. In 1926, the first Swiss canton passed legislation that expanded cantonal fire insurers to cover such disasters. Thus, the first Swiss PGE was established; a public insurer largely motivated by solidarity, which meant assuming collective responsibility for disasters. While opponents argued that the lack of statistical and mathematical basis made this novel solution a "jump into the unknown,"[3] it enabled protection against disasters that people were vulnerable to, which were previously considered uninsurable.

Other early PGEs, such as Caisse Centrale de Réassurance (CCR) in France (see Chapter 3) or the Earthquake Commission (EQC) in New Zealand (see Chapter 1), were also country-specific responses to disasters that the insurance industry deemed too unknowable to calculate and cover profitably. While these early PGEs have different objectives, interests, and governance structures, they all originated because insurance seemed a relevant and useful tool for protection from disaster, but there was not enough knowledge to sustain private-sector provision. As a response to this knowledge problem, they assumed some collective societal responsibility toward disasters arising from government intervention in the insurance market.

Rather than leaving individual citizens and the government with the inevitable burden of bearing some or all post-disaster losses, some form of government-backed insurance that could ease some of that burden was an appealing middle ground. As one industry expert reflected: "the pools were set up at that time. They were a necessary and appropriate reaction because the insurance industry was not enough and so in a sense it meant that the government had to intercede." (Interview—Insurance Industry). These PGEs provided insurance despite a lack of knowledge to calculate the risk (see Figure 2.1). There was often insufficient knowledge of three key components of calculating the risk of a disaster such as flood: knowledge about the nature of flood as a disaster (e.g., the probabilities of floods of different severity occurring at different locations), the exposure of property to flood (e.g., the building materials, property values, and replacement cost for different buildings at those locations), and the vulnerability of property to flood (e.g., the level of damage which would be expected from floods of different severity on different properties).

These PGEs faced a fundamental challenge: how to work with the disequilibrium occasioned by too little knowledge for these disasters to be insurable in the private market. They addressed this challenge by finding a way to ignore the lack of knowledge (see Figure 2.1: "ignoring too little knowledge"). These early PGEs relied heavily on redistributing disaster risk among the widest possible pool of citizens regardless of their individual risk profiles

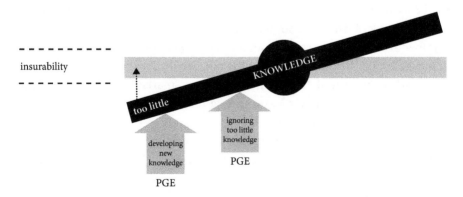

Figure 2.1 Origination of early PGEs in response to too little knowledge of disasters.

(see Chapter 1 and Appendix A). Typically, they instated compulsory insurance, collecting premiums across the population and thus creating a big enough pool of premiums for these PGEs to spread the risk of a loss across society (see more in Chapter 3).

This collective approach of spreading risk across society allowed these PGEs to generate an understanding of the aggregate losses they might face. However, it also limited their motivation to develop detailed knowledge about the risk affecting individual properties. As one PGE manager explained "we developed some internal modeling and we also used external ones. And the conclusion was … that according to our financial capacity we are going to cover all the disaster in [our country]" (Interview—PGE). Another PGE manager explained that, if they know they can cover the maximum losses, more detailed knowledge is not necessary. This is because price "is not based on the actual premium [for the risk level of the policyholder], it's based on [percentage of] the insurance capital. That's why it's the same for everyone" (Interview—PGE). Over time these PGEs also developed detailed knowledge to understand individuals' risk and their associated losses better, as depicted in "developing new knowledge" in Figure 2.1. But when they first originated, they came about because knowledge was simply too little to ensure insurability in a private market. Their key job was to find ways around that lack of knowledge.

2.3 And then we thought we knew: The origination of later PGEs

Advancements in knowledge have gradually expanded the insurability of disasters. This includes the scientific understanding of disasters, developments in the systematic application of statistical and actuarial techniques, and a growing body of data on insurance losses.[4] For many disasters in a growing number of regions, there was enough knowledge to build sufficient accuracy about potential losses that insurers felt confident to trade in these disasters in a market for a profit. Today, this process of "marketization" makes capital readily available to cover losses from a range of disasters such as floods, earthquakes, or terrorist attacks.

Yet, this knowledge, or perception of knowledge, is not settled.[5] Let's think about the 2001 World Trade Center terrorist attacks (9/11). In addition to thousands of fatalities and injuries this terrorist attack also had huge economic consequences. The total insured losses were some $32.5bn:[6] the largest-ever insurance loss at the time. The insurance industry as a whole was caught off guard. This type of attack had not previously been considered in insurance pricing.[7] Insured losses spanned multiple categories of insurance that were normally considered separately, including business interruption, property, liability, and workers' compensation.[8] The 9/11 attacks made the insurance industry understand that terrorism disasters could compound losses, resulting in claims beyond anything previously envisaged. While insurers and reinsurers managed to pay the claims, the attack resulted in an ongoing crisis that made the industry rethink the future of terrorism insurance. What the industry knew about terrorism risk, and their ability to measure and price it, changed overnight.

This sudden realization of the inadequacy of current knowledge made terrorism de facto uninsurable. Widespread terrorism exclusions in insurance policies were introduced. Most reinsurers (firms that provide insurance protection to insurance companies) withdrew from offering terrorism coverage. In turn, insurers withdrew as they could not carry the risk without reinsurance backing. The insurance system moved suddenly from equilibrium to disequilibrium. As one industry expert remembers: "you basically saw the industry very, very quickly starting to run away from it ... Everything was in complete disarray. Insurers could not do it because it was just too much exposure. Companies just started to pull out and they were not renewing their business" (Interview—Insurance Industry). Everybody was sure that the insurance industry could not survive another 9/11. The 9/11 attack pushed terrorism outside of the boundaries of existing knowledge and expectations for the insurance industry, and thus challenged the boundaries of insurability. Insurers lacked the knowledge to estimate the potential correlation and aggregate level of losses from a major terrorist attack. Without the ability to effectively calculate terrorism risk, in tandem with the realization that these incalculable losses were potentially enormous, their capacity to trade it for a profit was also in doubt. As a manager in one of the several terrorism PGEs formed after 9/11 later reflected, "reinsurers believed quite rightly that the underwriting of terrorism risk is probably not going to be profitable, in fact, it's probably uninsurable" (Interview—PGE). That is, uninsurable on insurance industry terms.

The 9/11 attacks making terrorism cover uninsurable provoked a societal crisis. As one insurer recalled, there was a complete halt to construction projects in New York City just as people were scrambling to rebuild: "if you were a property owner in New York City, you could not really get [terrorism] insurance. Construction projects just stalled ... All this had a huge negative impact on the economy. It was a very noticeable thing." (Interview—Insurance Industry). The widespread economic consequences of the sudden uninsurability of terrorism led to intervention by the US government. In discussion with the insurance industry, they established the Terrorism Risk Insurance Act (TRIA) in November 2002. A terrorism PGE for the US was born. TRIA counteracted the sudden disequilibrium in the knowledge paradox and made a new balance possible. It established conditions that made it possible to trade terrorism risk by ignoring what is not known, similar to the earlier PGEs already discussed. Through TRIA, the federal government would step in once terrorism losses to the insurance industry reached a specified aggregate level in any calendar year. Claims on any "unknowable" losses beyond that level would be paid by federal government capital reserves. In this way, the industry regained sufficient certainty about their maximum losses to be able to calculate suitable premiums and thereby continue to trade. The government meanwhile would not retain this loss over the long term. Rather, after a disaster, when the full cost of the claims was known and had been paid, the government would charge a levy on all insurance policies to recoup the money it had paid out.[9] The government thus intervened in the market process to provide the capital guarantee that insurers needed to continue operating. This intervention by the government supported the continued availability of terrorism insurance needed to allow businesses to function.

Like TRIA, other PGEs—such as Australian Reinsurance Pool Corporation (terrorism, Australia), California Earthquake Authority (earthquake, California), GAREAT (terrorism, France), and Pool Re (terrorism, UK)—were established in the face of a sudden withdrawal of insurance arising from an unexpected disaster that created an imbalance in the knowledge paradox (see Figure 2.2). These PGEs make uninsurable risk insurable again by ignoring the lack of knowledge that makes these disasters too hard to price and trade in the private market (see Figure 2.2: "ignoring too little knowledge"). To do so, they remove the unknown extremes of that risk from the insurance industry to the PGE, which assumes responsibility to pay for the claims, often with recourse to the government as the underpinning source of capital (see more in Chapter 3).

Over time the insurance industry may develop sufficient knowledge to calculate and price these disasters, and begin to bring in some of their own capital to insure the risk of loss (see Figure 2.2: "developing new knowledge"). However, when disaster losses remain largely unknown, PGEs become essential to the market functioning. For instance, TRIA has undergone several reviews over the years to reduce the government's exposure to terrorism risk (see Case 1.1). But it has not been phased out despite the US government's preference to do so. Rather, a new equilibrium has been created where the

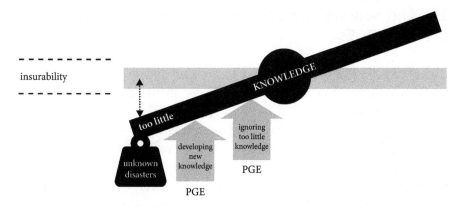

Figure 2.2 Origination of later PGEs in response to unknown disasters.

government continues to provide a safety net to cover some level of terrorism risk, allowing a capped remainder to be insurable again in the private sector. For insurers, terrorism risk remains too unknowable to be fully insured in a private market:

> Terrorism is so volatile, and the marketplace is a result of this. It's very difficult for the insurance market to control that volatility. … Probably, we will always need a government [backstop] to some extent, at least for the mega-catastrophic risk. It's just a matter of what level you need them.
>
> **(Interview—Insurance Industry)**

While 9/11 was geographically localized within the financial district of New York, it had global ramifications and similar situations of sudden uninsurability of terrorism risk arose around the globe. In France, insurers were required to provide terrorism cover as part of their fire policies. As the insurance industry found it impossible to offer terrorism insurance post-9/11, the ability of property owners in France to get *any* type of insurance cover was threatened by a large-scale "pull out" from the French property market. GAREAT was established on January 1, 2002 and was the first terrorism PGE following 9/11 to prevent a large-scale private-sector withdrawal. Other public-private solutions were also established rapidly, including the Australian Reinsurance Pool Corporation (ARPC). Each of these PGEs enables insurers to ignore the lack of knowledge about terrorism risk that would otherwise make it uninsurable in a private market. By using various forms of government guarantee to limit the maximum loss that the industry may face, these PGEs enable a market for terrorism insurance to persist.

2.4 And now we know too much: The origination of recent PGEs

For a long time, PGEs originated to resolve the problem of too little knowledge—either the absence of knowledge in the early twentieth century or recognition of the inadequacy of knowledge following later disasters. However, most recent PGEs have originated because of more frequent and severe weather-based disasters intersecting with improved modeling. Combined, these factors lead to too much knowledge for the insurance industry to provide insurance to properties at increasingly certain risk of disaster.

Let's explore the implications of this. The insurance industry is well-equipped to understand and trade in recurring disasters such as a flood in Paris, or a hurricane in Florida: their probability and frequency of occurrence as well as the aggregate level of losses can be calculated. Advancements in the relevant science (e.g., hydrology for flooding or geoscience for cyclones) and a much richer field of data available for calculation, have given insurance companies a growing ability to pinpoint which specific properties will be affected more.[10] For instance, the insurance industry absorbed the losses from frequent and devastating floods that occurred in the UK in the 2000s and early 2010s. However, afterward, premiums went up for properties that were classified as high-risk, with often-staggering increases. One elderly homeowner saw her home insurance soar from £267 to £1,767 (US $475 to US $3,145) in just a year—a nearly six-fold increase.[11] Other situations were even worse, with an increase of almost 900 percent in a matter of a few years.[12]

Homeowners were falling victim to the combined effects of more frequent and severe flooding and revised modeling. Flood losses provided an abundance of data, while better techniques allowed insurers to assess the risk of flooding per individual house with greater accuracy. In what is known as risk-reflective pricing, properties that insurers identified as being at high-risk of flooding were then charged very high premiums to reflect their greater risk of loss. Risk-reflective pricing is considered a sound actuarial practice that signals the cost of risk and enables insurers to remain solvent to pay claims.[13] However, it also means that many homeowners find their insurance premiums becoming unaffordable: "there are properties out there that aren't currently insured ... because they're too expensive" (Interview—Insurance Industry). As the likelihood of loss becomes almost certain for these homeowners, the insurance industry either no longer offers them insurance or charges them unaffordable premiums. Thus, in contrast to the 9/11 terrorist attacks, "too much knowledge" about disasters can also result in uninsurability.

Uninsurability arising from too much knowledge is a widespread pattern, emerging globally. Similar issues are occurring with cyclone insurance in Australia where "homeowners and businesses have been faced with crippling insurance costs, and in some cases, can't get insurance at all."[14] While most UK or Australian properties may remain insurable against floods and cyclones, high-risk policyholders are increasingly being "priced out" based on risk-reflective pricing. For instance, for some areas in Australia that are prone to flooding "the premium will be in the many thousands of dollars" (Interview—Government).

Unaffordability arising from too much knowledge is, therefore, another typical way that PGEs originate. Unlike the case of the sudden loss of confidence in existing knowledge, the shift from equilibrium to disequilibrium is not marked by a sudden insurance industry withdrawal. It occurs gradually, as a series of known and expected disasters, such as repeated floods, make insurance premiums unaffordable, and, thus, a particular subset of the population uninsurable (see Figure 2.3: "repeated disasters"). The number of high-risk properties becoming uninsurable steadily increases for various reasons, including more extreme weather and increased urbanization in areas at greater risk of disasters from that weather. Over years of such repeated disasters, the uninsured population increases, until the problem of uninsurability gains traction across society at large, becoming recognized as a societal crisis. Different stakeholders, including government and the insurance industry, then engage in ongoing discussions about how to address such issues.

For instance, following recurrent flooding in the UK, representatives from government, the Environment Agency, the insurance industry, and related

Figure 2.3 Origination of recent PGEs in response to too much knowledge of repeated disasters.

organizations worked together to develop a solution. The uninsurability of high-risk properties was recognized as a potential crisis: "the spirit in which a solution was set up was a hands-up acknowledgment that the market had failed for a certain group of customers, and there was a clear social need to do something about it" (Interview—Insurance Industry). Negotiations between the government and the insurance industry were heated. Insurers preferred to keep control over a free market where they could decide which risks made sense to trade commercially, and at what price. Government wanted to assert more control to ensure affordable prices for all properties, irrespective of the risk they bear. Amidst such contestation, a PGE, Flood Re, was launched in 2015 to address the problem. Legislated by the government, Flood Re deals with uninsurability by collecting a small levy on all residential policyholders. This levy provides Flood Re with a pot of premium that can be used to subsidize the cost of premiums to those at high-risk of flood, making their insurance more affordable. This process redistributes the risk of loss from high-risk policyholders across the wider pool of policyholders nationally.

This redistribution rebalances the knowledge paradox by allowing Flood Re to ignore knowledge of high-risk properties' specific flood risk when pricing flood insurance policies. The levy also alters the balance of the responsibility paradox away from risk-reflective premiums for individuals toward some collective responsibility for losses across the insured population of the UK. These changes, brought about by increasing government control over the market, have enabled the high premiums that would have been charged by the private sector to be reduced to a level that is affordable for individuals.

PGEs can thus originate as a societal answer to problems in the marketization of risk. In contexts of too much knowledge, the knowledge paradox becomes imbalanced, making risk uninsurable for a segment of the population. PGEs need to resolve this disequilibrium to provide insurance at an affordable price. Flood Re keeps further developing knowledge around flood risk for several reasons, including to influence flood resilience (see Chapter 5). Yet, when pricing insurance policies, it must overlook detailed knowledge about individual high-risk policyholders in order to redistribute their risk across the UK population (see Figure 2.3: "ignoring too much knowledge"). From a situation of disequilibrium PGEs, such as Flood Re, create a new equilibrium that prioritizes insurability over the risk-reflective pricing that would prevail in a market where control is given primarily to the insurance industry.

2.5 Are we always motivated to know? The origination of PGEs for disaster response

Governments with advanced economies typically have the funds to finance disaster response. Those with fragile economies often do not.[15] Such governments are typically dependent on humanitarian efforts and aid, which can be slow to mobilize in response to disasters. Disasters such as a hurricane in Haiti or a drought in Mali expose a different protection gap issue to that discussed above for individuals who cannot get insurance for property reconstruction. Rather, it is a gap between a country's need for rapid financial response to disaster, and the ability of the government of a country to meet the costs of that response themselves. We call this a disaster-response protection gap. Increasingly, insurance has been recognized as a means through which such governments can gain the capital and autonomy to finance some of this disaster response rather than waiting for international aid organizations.[16]

To bridge this disaster-response protection gap, several countries may come together to form a multi-country PGE. That is, a collective pool of countries, within which each individual country can gain some form of insurance protection. The multi-country PGE comprises a collective pot of operating capital, administrative and modeling capability, and geographic spread of risk that enables each country within it to buy an insurance product for disaster response that is underwritten by the global reinsurance industry (see Appendix A).[17] Examples of such PGEs are the Caribbean Catastrophe Risk Insurance Facility (CCRIF SPC) and the African Risk Capacity (ARC) which were established in 2007 and 2012 respectively. Alongside the countries themselves, development organizations like the World Bank and humanitarian organizations like the World Food Program collaborate in developing these PGEs, as part of their interest in supporting countries to build capability to respond to disasters.

PGEs are necessary to address a different knowledge problem in these contexts. Scientific knowledge about hurricanes or earthquakes is now significant. However, there is relatively little knowledge of how to model their effects or price the damage they cause in regions that have, historically, had little insurance, such as the Caribbean or the Pacific. The absence of knowledge here is not the same as in the first half of the twentieth century (see section 2.2), as the tools to assess and price risk are now available. While insurance has sophisticated expertise to calculate homeowners' losses from a hurricane hitting the coast of Florida, it has not fully transferred and adapted this knowledge to the Caribbean context, partly because data about historic losses are much scarcer in that context. This is a bit of a catch-22 situation. In what is termed low insurance penetration and demand, few people have or are looking to buy insurance in developing and newly developed economies. Low insurance penetration and demand mean a small market for insurers. Insurers thus have little incentive to develop the knowledge necessary to devise products specific to such regions, because they will not generate profit. However, the lack of products means that penetration remains low, generating a self-reinforcing cycle of disequilibrium, in which insurance in a private market is not available due to a lack of knowledge. Uninsurability therefore persists and affects the ability of the governments of these countries to buy insurance for themselves.

How disaster-response protection gaps emerge and are addressed in these contexts is similar to the process we described for early twentieth-century PGEs. First, a widely recognized societal crisis emerges. In the case of CRIFF's origination:

> You had Hurricane Ivan which struck a number of countries in the Caribbean ... And the losses for some countries were put at over two hundred percent of their GDP—I mean could you just imagine this? ... So you have this single event going through the Caribbean and causing this level of damage. So that really was a wakeup call for the governments of the Caribbean, who obviously realized they were very exposed to the advent of natural disasters like tropical cyclones, earthquakes and so on. So they decided that they needed to do something about it, so they enlisted the assistance of the World Bank.
>
> **(Interview—PGE)**

The Caribbean governments decided that they needed some form of insurance cover that would provide them with immediate cash flow—"liquidity"—in case of a major hurricane or earthquake, as no country could build significant reserves to respond to such a disaster. It was not economical for any single country to look at buying insurance cover individually. Rather, since on average one to three Caribbean countries are affected by a hurricane or an earthquake in any given year,[18] the Caribbean governments and their World Bank collaborators understood that a collective, pooled insurance solution would be the most cost-effective. This established the basis for a multi-country PGE.

However, the problem of uninsurability arose. Neither the countries, the development organizations, nor the insurance companies had models for developing insurance products for the Caribbean. As one participant explained, there was a lack of knowledge: "it was how do you develop it when the data are so bad and—well the data are bad because most of the countries did not have very long or good quality time series of data on that disaster. So, you know, how do you build a model and how do you test it?" (Interview— Development Agency). To generate insurance products that could move risk in these countries from the zone of uninsurability (too little knowledge) into the zone of insurability (sufficient knowledge), new knowledge needed to be developed to balance the knowledge paradox (see Figure 2.4, 1). As private insurers did not have a profit incentive to make a market to insure these developing countries, donors, development organizations, and the countries themselves chose to develop CCRIF as a response to societal demands to enhance disaster protection for such countries.

In some of our other examples PGEs enabled insurability by basically ignoring a lack of knowledge. By contrast, PGEs like CCRIF and ARC act as the vehicles for generating some of the knowledge necessary to make insurability possible. As a PGE manager explained, they collaborated with other stakeholders to find ways to estimate damage that did not rely heavily on historical insurance data; "we came up with a model of how it was going to work and that did take a while and a lot of consulting and talking to people" (Interview—PGE). They then developed models and novel insurance products that provided an urgent capital injection immediately after a disaster, rather than traditional insurance products that pay for reconstruction. These products, known as disaster liquidity insurance, were innovations in

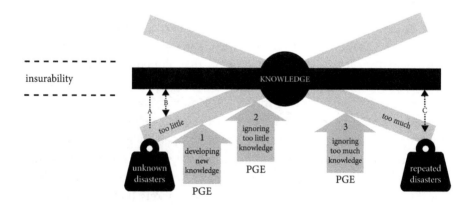

A: early PGEs (and multi-country PGEs in developing economies)
B: later PGEs
C: recent PGEs

Figure 2.4 PGE origination as a solution to the imbalances in the knowledge paradox.

insurance knowledge, as one participant explained; "it was quite revolution-ary because it provided liquidity. ... It would provide maybe three months of liquidity to those countries to continue paying their public servants, to ser-vice their debt, but it's not there to cover the loss" (Interview—Development Agency). This process of developing knowledge initiates the marketization of disaster in these countries by moving it from uninsurable to insurable. The PGEs act as the vehicle to enable that marketization.

2.6 Conclusion: The knowledge paradox, uninsurability, and PGE origination

Where there are imbalances in knowledge that restrict insurability the grounds are ripe for the formation of a PGE. It is tempting to imagine that insurance knowledge and disaster insurability have a linear relationship where an increase in one causes an increase in the other. However, as our dis-cussion of PGE origination has explained, the relationship between disaster insurance and the knowledge paradox—the tensions between too little and too much knowledge—is considerably more complex. We summarize this in Figure 2.4 and the rest of this section.

Historically, insurance has indeed worked to increase knowledge. As a result, flooding in Switzerland or France, to name but two examples, is now significantly more insurable than in the early twentieth century. The knowl-edge base has matured (see section 2.2). In those contexts, PGEs played a role in enabling insurability for disasters when knowledge was limited (Figure 2.4: A). They initially ignored the lack of knowledge (Figure 2.4: 2) through strategies of risk redistribution that altered the balance of the responsibility paradox, while at the same time supporting the gradual devel-opment of new knowledge (Figure 2.4: 1). However, too little knowledge is not simply a starting point that has now been left behind. While enough knowledge to insure disasters has been developed in many parts of the world, there are still many where the insurance market remains relatively underdeveloped. As we discussed in section 2.5, the private sector has his-torically chosen not to develop knowledge in markets that it has assessed as economically unattractive. Instead, governments and intergovernmental organizations have come together to develop PGEs, such as CCRIF in the Caribbean or ARC in Africa, that can be the focal point for a collective pool of country members to access insurance for disaster response. These PGEs build the knowledge necessary to develop insurance products that both serve the disaster needs of countries in the pool and also comprise an attractive proposition for insurers (Figure 2.4: 1).

In many parts of the world, and for many disasters, the lack of knowledge has been addressed. With increasing knowledge a robust insurance market has been developed. Yet knowledge about any type of disaster risk is not static (Figure 2.4: B). Disasters that are unexpected, either in nature or scale, can challenge existing knowledge, cause knowledge setbacks that erode insurability, or illustrate how little is still known about a disaster (see section 2.3, Figure 2.4: "unknown disasters"). Many PGEs have originated as a response to such knowledge setbacks, enabling the insurance market to persist by ignoring the lack of knowledge. For example, by ignoring the unknowability of terrorism risk in the UK, Pool Re has been able to offer insurance products that enabled the marketization of these disasters to continue. While these PGEs may develop knowledge to better understand these risks, they need to ignore the initial problem of too little knowledge. By doing so, they can price risk sufficiently to transfer it to their own balance sheets, which the private insurance industry is reluctant to do (Figure 2.4: 1 and 2).

At the other extreme, we have shown that it is possible to know too much. Repeated disasters with considerable losses (Figure 2.4: "repeated disasters") can result in "too much knowledge" about individual risk (Figure 2.4: C), pushing high-risk policyholders outside of insurability boundaries (see section 2.4). PGEs, like Flood Re in the UK, have altered the marketization of disaster risk by lowering premiums for high-risk policyholders—effectively ignoring their detailed knowledge of the risk of loss to those individuals (Figure 2.4: 3). They do this by subsidizing the premiums of those at high-risk and redistributing their disproportionate risk of a loss across the wider pool of policyholders, in this way reshaping the responsibility paradox.

PGEs originate to surmount these different imbalances in the knowledge paradox at the point when uninsurability has become a societal crisis that governments want to resolve. These PGEs can temporarily ignore too little or too much knowledge, to secure or restore insurability. In the longer term, PGEs can also support the development of knowledge (see Chapter 4) and use their knowledge productively to champion resilience measures that reduce the risk of disaster losses (see Chapter 5). This chapter explained why knowledge imbalances are associated with uninsurability and how PGEs work around those imbalances to make disaster risk insurable. As we show, the relationship between knowledge and insurability is dynamic and can suffer setbacks in what is known, or move into the problem of too much knowledge. PGEs thus remain important in addressing ongoing imbalances in the knowledge paradox.

2.7 Learning points

1. <u>PGE origination and the knowledge paradox.</u> To operate effectively, insurance needs balance between too much and too little knowledge of the risk of loss from a disaster. PGEs originate in contexts of disequilibrium where: (i) the knowledge paradox is unbalanced through too little or too much knowledge about a risk; (ii) knowledge imbalances lead to uninsurability, as private-sector insurance is either unaffordable or unavailable; and (iii) this uninsurability has prompted a societal crisis in which government intervenes in the market.

2. <u>PGEs as responses to the knowledge paradox:</u> The knowledge paradox is part of the problem (too little or too much knowledge) and the solution at origination. PGEs must: (i) ignore too little or too much knowledge; or (ii) develop new knowledge. In doing so, PGEs generate a new balance that enables hitherto uninsurable risk to be insured.

3. <u>PGEs involve government intervention in the insurance market.</u> PGEs come about because governments have intervened in the insurance market, putting the PGE in place to supplement or extend insurance beyond the insurance industry. PGEs are thus part of a new balance in government and industry control over the insurance market (see Chapter 1, section 1.4). This intervention can change responsibility for protection by: (i) removing risk from the insurance industry to the PGE and/or the government, so making them responsible to pay for losses; and/or (ii) redistributing risk from high-risk individuals across a wider group of policyholders.[19]

Notes

1. See Jarzabkowski, P., Chalkias, K., Cacciatori, E., Bednarek, R., *Between State and Market: Protection Gap Entities and Catastrophic Risk*. London: Cass Business School, City, University of London, 2018, 12–15. Available from: https://www.bayes.city.ac.uk/__data/assets/pdf_file/0020/420257/PGE-Report-FINAL.pdf.
2. Wanner, C., *Vorbeugen—Schützen—Entschädigen: Die entstehung der elementarschaden-versicherung in der Schweiz*. Bern: Historisches Institut—Universität Bern; 2002.
3. Wanner, *Vorbeugen*, 123.
4. Mitchell-Wallace, K., Jones, M., Hillier, J., Foote, M., *Natural Catastrophe Risk Management and Modelling: A Practitioner's Guide*. Hoboken, NJ: John Wiley & Sons; 2017.

RMS, "A Guide to Catastrophe Modelling." *The Review—Worldwide Reinsurance* (2008). Available from: https://forms2.rms.com/rs/729-DJX-565/images/rms_guide_catastrophe_modeling_2008.pdf.

Grossi, P., Kunreuther, H., eds. *Catastrophe Modeling: A New Approach to Managing Risk.* New York: Springer, 2005.

5. Taylor, Z. J., Weinkle, J. L. "The Riskscapes of Re/insurance." *Cambridge Journal of Regions, Economy and Society,* 13(2) (2020): 405–22. https://doi.org/10.1093/cjres/rsaa015

6. Insurance Information Institute, "Terrorism and Insurance: 13 Years after 9/11 the Threat of Terrorist Attack Remains Real." September 9, 2014. Available from: https://www.iii.org/press-release/terrorism-and-insurance-13-years-after-9-11-the-threat-of-terrorist-attack-remains-real-090914

7. Ericson, R., Doyle, A., "Catastrophe Risk, Insurance and Terrorism." *Economy and Society,* 33(2) (2004): 135–73. https://doi.org/10.1080/03085140410001677102

8. Hubbard, R. G., Deal, B., Hess, P., "The Economic Effects of Federal Participation in Terrorism Risk." *Risk Management and Insurance Review,* 8(2) (2004): 177–209. https://doi.org/10.1111/j.1540-6296.2005.00056.x

9. Michel-Kerjan, E., Kunreuther, H., "A Successful (Yet Somewhat Untested) Case of Disaster Financing: Terrorism Insurance under TRIA, 2002–2020." *Risk Management and Insurance Review,* 21(1) (2018): 157–80. https://doi.org/10.1111/rmir.12094.

Webel, B., *Terrorism Risk Insurance: Overview and Issue Analysis for the 116th Congress.* Report No.: R45707. Washington, DC: Congressional Research Service, December 27, 2019. Available from: https://crsreports.congress.gov/product/pdf/R/R45707

10. Boobier, T., *Analytics for Insurance: The Real Business of Big Data.* Hoboken, NJ: John Wiley & Sons, 2016, chapter 7, "Property insurance," 109–26. https://doi.org/10.1002/9781119316244.ch7.

Christophers, B., "The Allusive Market: Insurance of Flood Risk in Neoliberal Britain." *Economy and Society,* 48(1) (2019): 1–29. https://doi.org/10.1080/03085147.2018.1547494.

Taylor, Weinkle, "Riskscapes of re/insurance."

11. Hussain, A., "New Flood Maps Give Homeowners a Sinking Feeling as Cost of Insurance Soars." *The Times,* December 16, 2018. Available from: https://www.thetimes.co.uk/article/new-flood-maps-give-homeowners-a-sinking-feeling-as-cost-of-insurance-soars-35qlsgkfr

12. Gausden, G., "Pensioners' Home Insurance Soared from £300 to £3,300 in Four Years Due to Flood Risk, Even Though they'd Lived There for Four Decades." *This is Money,* May 19, 2019. Available from: https://www.thisismoney.co.uk/money/bills/article-7023045/Pensioners-home-insurance-soared-300-3-300-flood-risk.html

13. Landes, X., "How Fair Is Actuarial Fairness?" *Journal of Business Ethics,* 128(3) (2015): 519–33. https://doi.org/10.1007/s10551-014-2120-0

14. Khan, N., "Federal Government Announces Reinsurance Pool to Cover Cyclone Damage in Northern Australia." Australian Broadcasting Corporation, May 3, 2021. Available from: https://www.abc.net.au/news/2021-05-03/federal-government-reinsurance-pool-northern-australia/100113554

15. OECD, *Managing Risks in Fragile and Transitional Contexts: The Price of Success?* Paris: OECD Publishing, 2012. https://doi.org/10.1787/9789264118744-en.

Clarke, D., Wren-Lewis, L., *Solving Commitment Problems in Disaster Risk Finance.* Working paper no. 7720. Washington, DC: World Bank, 2016. Available from: https://openknowledge.worldbank.org/handle/10986/24638

16. Cummins, J. D., Mahul, O., *Catastrophe Risk Financing in Developing Countries: Principles for Public Intervention.* Washington, DC: World Bank Publications, 2009.

    Talbot, T., Dercon, S., Barder, O., *Payouts for Perils: How Insurance Can Radically Improve Emergency Aid.* Washington, DC: Center for Global Development, 2017. Available from: www.cgdev.org/node/312519.

    World Bank Group, *Disaster Risk Finance as a Tool for Development: A Summary of Findings from the Disaster Risk Finance Impact Analytics Project.* Washington, DC: World Bank; 2016. Available from: https://openknowledge.worldbank.org/handle/10986/24374

17. Jarzabkowski, P., Chalkias, K., Clarke, D., Iyahen, E., Stadtmueller, D., Zwick, A., *Insurance for Climate Adaptation: Opportunities and Limitations.* Rotterdam and Washington, DC: Global Commission on Adaptation, UN, 2019. Available from: https://www.insdevforum.org/wp-content/uploads/2020/08/Insurance-for-Climate-Adaptation-Opportunities-and-Limitations.pdf.

    Cummins, J. D., Mahul, O., *Catastrophe Risk Financing.*

18. Cummins, Mahul, *Catastrophe Risk Financing.*

19. See Jarzabkowski et al., *Between State and Market*, 12–15.

3

Shouldering the burden

Who controls the market and has responsibility for protection?

3.1 Introduction

The PGEs' remit—what they should achieve and how—shapes the different ways they engage with the question of uninsurability. We have shown that PGEs originate when the knowledge paradox becomes unbalanced—too much or too little is known about a particular risk, making it uninsurable (see Chapter 2). But PGEs are not self-initiated. They originate as the outcome of protracted and fraught negotiations about who should control the insurance market—the insurance industry or the government (the control paradox)— and whether individuals or society as a collective should be responsible for protection (the responsibility paradox). These negotiations result in remits that vary significantly across PGEs, depending on the specific facet of uninsurability that the PGE is meant to address (for example, the absence or sudden withdrawal of insurance or the creeping growth of unaffordability), and the social and political context. Each of these remits, however, shapes the extent to which a PGE can maneuver within the control and responsibility paradoxes.

First, a PGE's remit is defined by the extent of insurance industry or government control over how insurance protection is provided to society. All PGEs, even those that are controlled by the private insurance industry, come about through government legislation aimed at addressing some specific societal need for insurance. Yet all PGEs, even those that are government-owned or backed, also use an insurance industry-based system to collect premiums and pay for the losses from disasters. There are thus tensions between industry and government control that each PGE balances in different ways.

Second, a PGE's remit also broadly demarcates who is intended to be responsible for paying for protection from disaster; the specific individual at risk, or the broader collective of people within a society.[1] While individuals buy insurance, the insurance system depends on some collective spreading

Disaster Insurance Reimagined. Paula Jarzabkowski et al., Oxford University Press. © Paula Jarzabkowski, Konstantinos Chalkias, Eugenia Cacciatori, and Rebecca Bednarek (2023). DOI: 10.1093/oso/9780192865168.003.0003

of the responsibility to pay for losses.[2] Each individual buying insurance also pays in advance for a fraction of the losses of other individuals in the collective, regardless of whether they themselves make a claim. PGE encapsulate within their remit the extent to which individuals should bear responsibility for their potential losses or whether society assumes a collective approach to those losses.

We now examine three PGE examples: California Earthquake Authority (CEA), Caisse Centrale de Réassurance (CCR), and CCRIF (Caribbean Catastrophe Risk Insurance Facility). Each of these cases maneuvers within the parameters of these control and responsibility paradoxes differently. This is because, while all are intended to address some local issue of uninsurability, they have very different remits for doing so. At CEA the remit is to maintain as much insurance industry control over the market as possible and to ensure individuals remain responsible for their own protection. CCR's remit is defined by government control over the insurance market to ensure that it can provide collective disaster insurance protection for France. CCRIF occupies a middle ground within these two paradoxes. These variations occur because PGEs are not simply trying, universally, to rebalance competing demands over control and responsibility. Rather, they are acting on remits that have been defined differently, according to the problems that uninsurability causes for key stakeholders within their specific country or region.

In this chapter we explore these differences in PGEs' remits and the tensions that they bring about for these PGEs. We also discuss the implications of different remits for uninsurability. The questions that both shape and linger throughout this chapter are: What is the consequence of designing remits in a certain way? And what, if any, interplay arises between the way PGEs address local problems of uninsurability and the wider issue of uninsurable disasters?

3.2 Coupling industry control with individual responsibility: The case of CEA

The 1994 Northridge 6.7 magnitude earthquake in southern California caused insured losses of $14.5bn, which reportedly equated to more than 80 years of premiums for earthquake risk in California.[3] The magnitude of loss was a clear message to the insurance industry: existing pricing of earthquake risk did not reflect the actual risk. Earthquake risk was severely underpriced, and insurers were now facing large unexpected losses.

3.2.1 The remit of CEA

California law stipulated that insurers must offer earthquake cover to all homeowners as part of any residential property insurance product. Alarmed at the shocking losses incurred by the Northridge earthquake, insurers wanted to "shed that risk that is a requirement in the State" (Interview—Insurance Industry). Unable to offer any insurance unless they also offered earthquake insurance, the industry simply withdrew, or severely restricted the availability of insurance policies for properties. The societal impact of homeowner insurance withdrawal was significant. Californians could no longer insure their homes for any potential risk, not just earthquake. And homeowners cannot get a mortgage without a home insurance policy in place.

A local protection gap resulted for home insurance in California. Faced with a severe crisis, the state of California, led by the insurance commissioner, worked with the insurance industry to find a solution. The result was the California Earthquake Authority (CEA). Created in 1996 CEA is a privately funded, publicly managed, not-for-profit PGE built around a remit to "get the residential property insurance market back, simply because the real estate industry depends on them [homeowners] getting homeowners' insurance" (Interview—Insurance Industry).

CEA was legally obliged to offer and accept anyone who wanted to purchase earthquake insurance, no matter how high-risk their property: "if a person says … 'I really want earthquake insurance', we have to take them. The only reason we could turn someone away is if they have pre-existing earthquake damage" (Interview—PGE). This meant that the private market was able to continue to provide all other homeowner insurance, with the offer of earthquake insurance met by the CEA. CEA thus solved one specific aspect of the problem of uninsurability—lack of availability of insurance caused by the withdrawal of the insurance industry from the market.

3.2.2 Maneuvering within the control and responsibility paradoxes

CEA's remit supports industry control over the insurance market. Insurance protection continues to be delivered through the private sector, with CEA only there to provide the earthquake cover that private insurers were unwilling to offer. Individuals purchase earthquake insurance from CEA in return for a premium. CEA's remit enables industry control over the market to remain by ensuring that other forms of insurance protection, such as for fire, remained available within the private sector: "the goal of the CEA was to revive the residential property insurance market, period ... There was a great deal of effort put in to finding a way to avoid a government program and to simply have the market come back" (Interview—Insurance Industry). The insurance market in California remained industry-controlled, with CEA's intervention enabling that insurance market to persist.

This maintenance of industry control is entangled with conditions that dictate who should shoulder the burden of paying for protection; in this case, individuals. CEA is legally required to offer earthquake insurance to Californian homeowners, but the legislation that defines its remit stipulates that the price of the earthquake policies provided must reflect the degree of risk. This means that the cost of earthquake insurance is not shared across California homeowners. Rather, everyone is charged different premiums based on the risk that the individual bears: "it is not always responsible to simply average premiums" (Interview—PGE). CEA's pricing varies by individual, according to geographical variations in risk, building age, construction type, and the coverage amounts and deductibles selected: "it is really wide differential pricing ... the oldest homes and the most vulnerable homes in the most vulnerable locations are going to be charged at ... a pretty steep price" (Interview—PGE).

CEA originated to ensure that Californian society benefited from the provision of insurance protection and that homeowner insurance could continue to be offered. However, its remit meant that the protection is offered at a competitive risk-reflective price. The insurance market remains largely under industry control: even for earthquake insurance, there is no government back-stop or legislation for cross-subsidization that could enable prices to be smoothed across the whole society. Earthquake protection is instead the responsibility of the individual. Designing CEA in that way had certain implications.

3.2.3 Successes and challenges

CEA's managers successfully fulfilled its remit. CEA preserves the marketization of risk by ensuring the continuity of homeowners' insurance provision in California. It also ensures the availability of earthquake insurance, whilst leaving the affordability issue unresolved. Only about 10 percent of households in California had earthquake cover in 2019.[4] Furthermore, the ones buying earthquake cover are mostly those at lower risk: "the majority of our business is the low-risk, medium-risk [property owners], basically the ones for whom it is cheaper. Less than 17% of our portfolio is in the high-risk area" (Interview—PGE). In making individuals responsible for their risk, rather than decreasing the price of insurance for high-risk individuals, the CEA has been unable to address the problem that those individuals were finding "earthquake insurance unaffordable". They thus remain unprotected, leaving the problem of insurability only partially resolved.

CEA lives with this inherent problem. It is unable to provide affordable prices to those at high-risk because there is little government control of the market. There is no capped or unlimited government guarantee. Nor can CEA introduce mandatory earthquake insurance at a standard levy rate, to enable it to reduce prices: "they haven't brought in a solidarity model. They do have risk-reflective pricing, and as a result, they have very low insurance penetration" (Interview—Insurance Industry). CEA moved California from the disequilibrium of full uninsurability, restoring sufficient equilibrium that property insurance was available. Yet, it has little, if any, ability to redress the broader problem of earthquake uninsurability—which is represented in the fact that so few Californians are insured for earthquake today. Furthermore, there is little sociopolitical will to push for more government control that might enable greater collective responsibility for, and price reductions to, those most at risk. As not everyone in California is exposed to earthquakes, such an approach is considered unpalatable and unfair: "people would say to themselves why am I subsidizing someone else" (Interview—Insurance Industry).

3.3 Coupling government control with collective responsibility: The case of CCR

Historically, disasters such as floods or earthquakes were typically excluded from insurance policies in France. After more than a decade of discussion, the Natural Disaster compensation scheme was established in France in 1982 to address this issue of uninsurability for so-called "natural" disasters.

3.3.1 The remit of CCR

The compensation scheme, the state-owned Caisse Centrale de Reassurance (CCR), was established by the French government in the aftermath of World War II as the first reinsurance company in France.[5] As part of the scheme, CCR was given the power to deliver unlimited government-guaranteed reinsurance coverage for domestic insurance policies against disasters like

flood and earthquake, enabling their insurability. But it was not just the guarantee that addressed the widespread uninsurability of disasters within France.
CCR's remit is built primarily around collective responsibility, ensuring that
all French citizens are protected against disasters. This is achieved through
mandatory disaster insurance.

3.3.2 Maneuvering within the control and responsibility paradoxes

The French government requires all insurers to offer natural disaster insurance as part of any other insurance offering, such as fire. As part of this
government control over the market, everyone pays the same price for
the "Natural Catastrophe" premium surcharge within the policy,[6] regardless of their actual risk profile: "the rate of premium is absolutely the
same if you are in a disaster zone or a safe zone" (Interview—PGE).
In this way, CCR is, effectively, an "efficient mutualization of fifty million people and perhaps ten million business companies" (Interview—
PGE) that makes French society, collectively, responsible for disaster insurance protection. Insurers are not legally allowed to choose which risk
is included or excluded from an insurance policy (mandatory insurance
offer), and the premiums that they charge for disaster insurance are also
government-controlled.

Private insurers cannot simply be forced to offer insurance in this context, as they would potentially face crippling losses. This is where CCR steps
in, providing government support to ensure that the insurance industry can
function while offering disaster insurance. In a traditional commercial insurance market, insurers pay a premium to reinsurers, who in exchange pay a
share of the large-scale claims incurred by the insurers following a disaster.
This is a means by which insurance firms can insure themselves for large-scale
losses (see Appendix A). CCR, as a public-sector reinsurer, provides insurers
operating in France with unlimited reinsurance cover for these disaster risks
in exchange for a premium. In effect, CCR is a government reinsurer that uses
the private insurance market as a mechanism to pool risks and premiums to
provide French citizens and businesses with protection against disaster: "we
have a mission by the government to provide public reinsurance for natural
catastrophes" (Interview—PGE).

CCR's remit as a public entity with an unlimited guarantee enables the
government to control the insurance market's ability to provide disaster protection. But it remains a market. CCR draws on the private industry to deliver
its solution and it is not simply the state paying for disaster losses. Individuals

purchase insurance from the private sector, paying premiums to insurers, and a proportion of these premiums (alongside the respective risk of loss) is then transferred to CCR. This allows CCR to build up capital reserves that can then be used to support insurers with claims payments in the event of a major disaster loss. Thus, while the domestic insurance market is strongly controlled by the government, the insurance industry persists and individuals buy into industry-based insurance processes to access protection.

CCR's remit to build collective responsibility for disaster protection, underpinned by government control of the insurance market, contrasts with the industry control and individual responsibility incorporated in CEA's remit described in section 3.2. Yet, like CEA, in addressing uninsurability, CCR does not simply try to balance industry and government control and individual and collective responsibility for protection. Rather, CCR has created its own equilibrium, quite different from that of CEA, to ensure widespread, available, and affordable provision of disaster protection through a strongly government-controlled insurance market.

3.3.3 Successes and challenges

The fundamental assumption underpinning CCR's remit for government-controlled, mandatory insurance is widespread affordable protection for France. This collective approach is seen as the fairest way: "you have people who bought their house thirty years ago [when the extent of risk was not known]; and some areas are more exposed to one peril and others to another" (Interview—PGE). Without CCR, premiums would fluctuate across locations and policyholders, potentially making some high-risk areas uninsurable (see Chapter 2). For instance, Elodie, the owner of a flat in Marseille that has been flooded multiple times in recent years, would see her premiums rise significantly and be unable to afford to buy insurance anymore. Instead, the unlimited reinsurance guarantee provided by CCR ensures that insurers can afford to provide the uniformly affordable price on her policy that state regulations dictate: "I think the scheme of CCR, with that guarantee, is very important because you have equity between people, and we can cover Natural Catastrophe for an acceptable price" (Interview—PGE). The whole of the French domestic insurance market thus takes collective responsibility for the multiple risks that different individuals face.

This new equilibrium of government control and collective responsibility raises two key tensions. First, the private industry at times criticizes CCR for unfairly dominating the French "natural" disaster reinsurance market. CCR is not technically a monopoly: insurers can get reinsurance cover from any private reinsurer or even decide not to buy reinsurance at all. But most choose to transfer their risk to CCR because the unlimited guarantee provided by the government means CCR provides a more comprehensive offering: "we have, let's say, about 90 percent of the market" (Interview—PGE). Some private insurers feel restricted, arguing that, if they could charge more, private market capital could pay for losses in France: "the level of the original premium is not decided by us. We would like to retain a lot [more risk] if we were able to decide on the level of the premium charged to our clients" (Interview—Insurance Industry). With the current arrangement, private reinsurers also feel excluded, as private reinsurer SCOR stated: "the exclusive nature of this guarantee … gives CCR a de facto virtual monopoly, enabling it to control a market share of over 90 percent."[7] Generally, however, the insurance industry seems content to have CCR creating this new equilibrium in the system: "I think the scheme is, in the end, a good scheme because it allows people to be covered. Everybody to be covered, even the most exposed" (Interview—Insurance Industry). Since CCR builds on national solidarity to provide an efficient way of addressing the wider issue of uninsurability, its intervention appears justifiable to such insurers.

Second, there are tensions regarding how to manage the wide variation between individual risk profiles in the future. CCR has data showing that some areas are at increasingly high-risk. For instance, studies suggest that the extreme weather disaster claim rate in metropolitan France could double each year between now and 2050.[8] The risk-reflective pricing that we saw in CEA is one way in which the insurance market can signal the extent of a risk to society. The associated high insurance premiums can be an incentive for individuals and societies to minimize risk through mitigation measures. CCR has rejected risk-reflective pricing and instead uses the availability of its products to incentivize wider insurance cover.

CCR continues to smooth pricing so that people are not penalized for legacy risks over which they have no control, such as older houses that have now become flood-prone. However, it endeavors to curb future risks by differentiating insurance availability at both the individual and collective levels. For example, CCR excludes some cover for communes (local councils) that have not put in place risk-mitigation plans, so bringing a collective element to penalizing failure to control future risk (see Chapter 5 for more on disaster resilience). Neither does CCR insure new properties in exposed areas, an omission intended to disincentivize purchases in such areas.

Despite these tensions, CCR's remit remains focused on collective protection from disaster, supported by government control that ensures that the insurance market continues to function primarily for the benefit of society.

3.4 Incorporating individual and collective responsibility into an industry-government solution: The case of CCRIF

Some PGEs, like CEA and CCR, work at extremes of the control and responsibility paradoxes. Others take a middle ground position in maneuvering within these two paradoxes. We now explain one such example: a multi-country PGE, established with a remit to support countries with fragile economies to access insurance as part of their disaster response strategies.

3.4.1 The remit of CCRIF

In 2004 Hurricane Ivan devastated the Caribbean. It cost some countries over 200 percent of their GDP and damaged 95 percent of their housing stock.[9] This disaster was "a wake-up call for the governments of the Caribbean in terms of their exposure to natural catastrophe risk," and so "they decided that they needed to do something about it" (Interview—PGE). The governments turned to the World Bank for help: "so Caricom [an intergovernmental Caribbean Community organization of 15 member states] heads of State came to the bank and said: we can't go on like this, please help us figure out how to manage our risk better" (Interview—Development Agency). The result was that in 2007 the Caribbean Catastrophe Risk Insurance Facility (CCRIF), the world's first multi-country PGE, was formed under the technical leadership of the World Bank and with supporting funding from multiple donor countries outside the Caribbean.

CCRIF has a remit to "limit the financial impact of catastrophic hurricanes, earthquakes and excess rainfall events to Caribbean countries."[10] In fulfillment of its remit, CCRIF offers its member countries disaster liquidity insurance products that provide a rapid injection of cash—liquidity—to respond in the immediate aftermath of a disaster. Such disaster liquidity within days of a disaster is crucial in averting the escalation of the crisis. For example, early response to drought can halve the number of livestock deaths and is 14 times cheaper than the cost of replacing dead livestock as part of a slower aid-relief response.[11]

Unlike traditional insurance, such as that offered by the CEA and CCR, which is for the reconstruction of impacted properties, disaster liquidity insurance is solely for urgent disaster response to help make people safe and stabilize the situation. It is not sufficient to fund reconstruction and this is not its aim. Products to cover the full cost of reconstruction would be extremely expensive given that the scale of some disasters in such countries can be in the magnitude of their entire GDP. Because they do not endeavor to cover the costs of reconstruction, disaster liquidity products are more affordable, which is important since these are mostly countries with restricted budgets. In addition, as explained in Chapter 2, because they pay rapidly disaster liquidity products address an important protection gap between the aftermath of disaster and the time taken for humanitarian and other forms of disaster relief to be mobilized. Specifically, these are "parametric" insurance products on which payment is triggered based on particular predefined, contractually agreed parameters, such as the type, severity, and location of a disaster. For example, for a hurricane disaster liquidity product the trigger could be a specific wind speed recorded within a defined geographical location. When these triggers are met—the wind blows at that speed in that place—there is no need for any lengthy claims process. Rather, immediate payouts are issued to help with urgent disaster response, such as restoring power supply or providing food and temporary shelter. The insurance payments are thus an important part of a wider ecosystem of response that includes international aid and debt-based financing.[12]

CCRIF functions as a not-for-profit insurance facility that works with and for those governments of Caribbean countries that are participating members. Each of these countries pays their own individual premium based on the risk profile of their country, and the amount of cover they wish to have to respond to disaster in their country. CCRIF serves as the collective pooling mechanism for these individual countries. It combines the benefits of pooled reserves from the participating countries with the financial capacity of the international insurance industry. In short, CCRIF retains some of the risk transferred by the participating countries and then transfers the remainder of the risk to the private reinsurance industry. CCRIF buys these reinsurance products centrally every year to cover all the Caribbean countries paying premiums to be part of the pool. This structure allows the member countries to take advantage of pooled technical capabilities to help structure their insurance products. They can also buy disaster cover more cost effectively than if they tried to get reinsurance cover on their own.[13] Then, for any country that suffers a disaster that meets the predefined triggering criteria, CCRIF, drawing from the private industry capital, will issue a rapid payment of the predefined amount agreed with that country member.

As CCRIF relies on the insurance industry to provide this insurance capital, these disaster liquidity products need to be viable in a global insurance market. As explained in Chapter 2, the amount of revenue that such products provide is not sufficient to encourage the private sector to develop these products independently or to develop the risk pooling system across countries that makes them affordable to each country. One such PGE explained that developing these products is "incredibly expensive, right, and no private sector company is going to do this unless they're guaranteed the transaction at the end of the day" (Interview—PGE). Nonetheless, the private industry is happy to be involved in providing the capital once the products are in place, if the approach is economically viable: "working to an actual market model. That is sustainable because the industry will always be there if you pay the premium that it asks for" (Interview—Insurance Industry).

3.4.2 Maneuvering within the control and responsibility paradoxes

CCRIF is thus a PGE that provides insurance protection that falls under the control of both the participating governments and the insurance industry. While insurers benefit from their ability to access a new market, CCRIF's primary remit is to serve the disaster risk management and protection needs of the member governments. Hence, CCRIF is at least partially controlled by the governments of the participating countries, as it is acting on their and, ultimately, their citizens' behalf. Indeed, CCRIF is a means of ensuring that non-market-based values are pursued through the insurance market, such as countries' duty of protection to their citizens, or values of regional solidarity amongst countries to protect those that are more vulnerable. For instance, CCIRF sometimes uses donors and its own funding to offer discounted premiums or even pay premiums in full for some of its very low-income country members, which would be impossible if the insurance cover was fully controlled by the private sector. CCRIF's goal is not to make profits but to build some level of protection for society through insurance against the financial instability and devastation that disasters can bring. However, the protection it offers is also controlled by the insurance industry. The capital to pay for disasters is provided by the insurance industry, which will only trade in risk that is economically viable and meets at least some level of profitability (see Appendix A). CCRIF thus negotiates a position between government and industry control to deliver its remit.

CCRIF's remit also requires it to accommodate both individual and collective responsibility for protection. On the one hand, as with any typical insurance transaction, each individual country is a policyholder whose government decides if they need protection, at what level, and how much they are prepared to pay for it. If these governments feel that their countries' interests are unmet they may leave the pool: "the value proposition has to be very strong for a Minister to agree to spend every year something where the return on their payments may be, by definition, zero for every year when there is no disaster" (Interview—Development Agency). Each individual country thus decides annually if membership in the pool still meets its interests. On the other hand, CCRIF needs to ensure that the pool will remain large enough for insurance to remain viable by building a sense of collective responsibility for protection across its members. While each country is responsible for managing its own risks and paying for its cover, CCRIF also takes actions that promote collective responsibility for protection across the region. For instance, CCRIF sometimes offers help with premiums to very low-income countries, enabling them to stay in the pool even if they cannot assume full responsibility for paying their premiums. It also funds disaster-risk management and mitigation projects for countries and supports risk-management education programs. These activities build collective responsibility about risk across the Caribbean—reflected in the fact that most countries have remained members over the years, even though they do not always receive payouts.

CCRIF has thus created a new equilibrium that enables disaster liquidity insurance to be provided by balancing government and industry control, and individual and collective responsibility.

3.4.3 Successes and challenges

CCRIF successfully fulfills its remit by ensuring the widespread and affordable provision of disaster-liquidity insurance for governments across the Caribbean. In fact, between its inception in 2007 and 2021, CCRIF has made 54 payouts totaling US $245 million to 16 member countries. All payouts have been made within 14 days of a disaster, with some governments receiving partial payouts within five to seven days to begin recovery efforts and to support their most vulnerable citizens.[14] These payouts have helped its country members fund their disaster response in the immediate aftermath of several major disasters. Referring to one such payout, a CCRIF manager explained: "we knew, for example, how many people this single payout has helped—you could say 140,000 people—the medication that was purchased, the number of roofs that were built" (Interview—PGE). A prime minister of another country explained the value of the payout they received: "this cheque will be going directly to strengthening and rebuilding our agriculture sector."[15]

CCRIF addresses a specific, focused problem of disaster-response liquidity for its member countries. However, its remit is not addressing the wider uninsurability of disaster risk in these countries where the insurance market is not well-developed. CCRIF was not designed to address widespread and comprehensive reconstruction post-disaster or the lack of homeowner insurance more generally amongst the population. Indeed, this wider social issue of uninsurability remains largely unresolved in these societies, even as they bear the brunt of climate change in terms of disaster risk.

3.5 Conclusion: PGEs expand the possibilities for equilibrium

There are many ways for a PGE to fulfill its remit. Compared to the traditional insurance industry, PGEs expand the possibilities for equilibrium. As depicted in Figure 3.1, they do so by combining the poles of industry or government control over the market (horizontal axis) and individual or collective responsibility for protection (vertical axis) in multiple ways.

To deliver their remits and build a new equilibrium within which insurability is possible, some PGEs prioritize one or the other end of the control

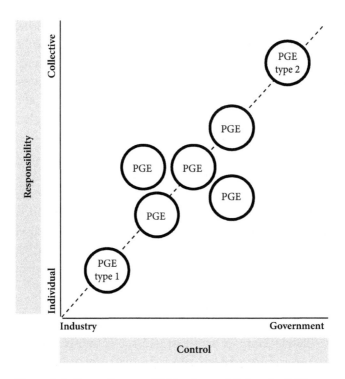

Figure 3.1 Expanding possibilities for equilibrium for PGEs with different remits.

and responsibility paradoxes. Either through privileging industry control and individual responsibility (Figure 3.1, PGE Type 1), or government control and collective responsibility (Figure 3.1, PGE Type 2). Across the PGEs that comprise our dataset (see Appendix B), we did not observe PGEs with remits where government control bundled strongly with individual responsibility or industry control with collective responsibility. This is because when insurance protection falls under industry control then responsibility for protection typically resides with individuals, holding them responsible for paying premiums at a risk-reflective price. By contrast, when insurance protection falls under government control, then responsibility for risk resides mostly with the collective, as the government can distribute the potential for losses across a society. Hence, as shown in Figure 3.1, most PGEs cluster along the dotted line, building insurability by combining the elements of the two paradoxes in ways that occupy a middle ground between them, as with our example of CCRIF (section 3.4).

How a PGE maneuvers within the control and responsibility paradoxes is not an arbitrary decision. It depends on the PGE's remit—the problem it was originally set up to solve and how it was mandated to address it. This remit is also shaped by the sociopolitical and cultural system within which the PGE is embedded and the historical moment in which it originates. In highly marketized contexts that abhor government intervention in markets[16] and in highly individualistic contexts,[17] remits such as that of the CEA tend to prevail. That is, remits focused on maintaining industry control over the market and ensuring that individuals take responsibility for their own protection. By contrast, in countries with a culture of solidarity, a remit to maximize social protection through government control over the market is more likely, as in CCR's case. Alternatively, as with the CCRIF case, a PGE might aim to find a flexible balance, combining industry and government control and subsidizing some higher-risk or less-fortunate members to bring them into the collective even as it focuses on individual responsibility for the others. Regardless, all PGEs work to address the disequilibrium that is causing uninsurability in their own local contexts, discharging their various remits in ways that expand the possibilities for equilibrium in that context.

The way that a PGE fulfills its remit has implications for the very issue of uninsurability. Those that privilege industry control and individual responsibility tend to have less impact on the wider issue of uninsurability than PGEs that privilege government control and collective responsibility. For example, the CEA addressed the availability but not the affordability issue that made risk uninsurable, whereas CCR was able to address both.

This is not, however, an argument to design all PGEs with government control and collective responsibility. There are always trade-offs. For example, risk-reflective pricing, which arises from the PGE Type 1 position (Figure 3.1), provides pricing signals that a particular area is highly prone to disaster, which may indicate that it is not viable for people to continue to live there and/or that mitigation efforts are needed (such as better building codes). These pricing signals are suppressed by the collective responsibility that characterizes government-controlled PGEs (Figure 3.1, PGE Type 2), potentially masking the decreasing viability of some areas. This is important when we consider issues of physical resilience to disaster, which we explore further in Chapter 5.

Sociopolitical realities also need to be considered. Government-controlled PGEs require a strong political commitment and often an accompanying financial guarantee by governments. And a PGE founded on the principle of collective responsibility for risk requires a national or regional culture of solidarity.[18] In short, PGEs and their remits reflect the local society from which they emerge: what is possible in France may not be possible in California. Nonetheless, lessons can be learned from greater awareness of the trade-offs involved.

This issue of ongoing wrestling with the boundaries of a PGE's remit leaves us with an as-yet unanswered, question. This chapter has shown that PGEs are designed to solve a local problem arising from their origination at a specific point in time. Should the remit of PGEs be limited to fixing the initial problem, or should it have the flexibility to evolve as disasters, their insurability, and stakeholders' expectations for protection evolve? And how might PGEs navigate this issue? We pick up this question in the next chapter.

3.6 Learning points

1. <u>The design of a PGE's remit aligns with the local problem it is brought about to solve.</u> There is no one-size-fits-all design that should be used by PGEs to address issues of uninsurability. Apart from the sociopolitical context within which PGEs operate, the key reason for variation is based on the specific nature of the problem they are asked to solve. For instance, if the problem is restoring private-sector capital that has been withdrawn from some risk, a PGE remit that is focused on reinstating industry control over the market might resolve this problem. If the problem is maximizing societal protection across the entire population, then a PGE with a remit to build collective responsibility might

be preferred. Other problems might lend themselves to yet different remits, each of which might combine issues of control and responsibility differently, including providing controls that enable the subsidization of some high-risk parts of society, without moving toward full collective responsibility.

2. The design of a PGE's remit has implications for uninsurability. Different PGE remits are more or less effective at solving the affordability and availability components of uninsurability (see Chapter 1). While PGEs that privilege industry control and individual responsibility can successfully resolve the local problems they are confronted with at origination, the wider issue of uninsurability is often difficult to address. PGEs that balance industry with government control and individual with collective responsibility, and those that privilege government control and collective responsibility, will typically have a better result in increasing the availability and the affordability of insurance, so having a more profound effect on uninsurability, at least in the short term. However, as we will explore in Chapter 5, increasing the affordability of insurance blunts incentives to risk mitigation and can become problematic to sustain in the longer term.

Notes

1. Baker, T., Simon, J., eds, *Embracing Risk: The Changing Culture of Insurance and Responsibility*. Chicago: University of Chicago Press, 2002.

   Ericson, R. V., Doyle, A., Barry, D., *Insurance as Governance*. Toronto: University of Toronto Press, 2003.

2. Lehtonen, T. K., Liukko, J., "The Forms and Limits of Insurance Solidarity." *Journal of Business Ethics*, 103(1) (2011): 33–44. https://doi.org/10.1007/s10551-012-1221-x.

   Lehtonen, T. K., Liukko, J., "Producing Solidarity, Inequality and Exclusion through Insurance." *Res Publica*, 21(2) (2015): 155–69. https://doi.org/10.1007/s11158-015-9270-5

3. Reich, K., "Earthquake Insurance Agency Is Born." *Los Angeles Times*, September 28, 1996. Available from: https://www.latimes.com/archives/la-xpm-1996-09-28-mn-48246-story.html

4. Miller, N., "When it Comes to Earthquake Insurance, Only about 10 Percent of California Homes Are Covered." *Cap Radio*, July 9, 2019. Available from: https://www.capradio.org/articles/2019/07/09/when-it-comes-to-earthquake-insurance-only-about-10-percent-of-california-homes-are-covered/

5. Atlas Magazine, "Scor from 1970 up to Now." October 2010. Last updated May 20, 2013. Available from: https://www.atlas-mag.net/en/article/scor-from-1970-up-to-now

6. The premium surcharge is uniform and set by law: 12 percent of the base Fire rate for non-Auto policies and 6 percent for Auto Property Damage policies. The base rate itself is not regulated.

7. Reuters, "Reinsurer Scor Takes CCR Challenge to EU." September 27, 2013. Available from: https://www.reuters.com/article/idUKL5N0HN1S620130927

8. Moncoulon, D., "Impact of Climate Change on Natural Disaster Insurance in France." ConsorsSeguros, April 2016. Available from: https://www.consorsegurosdigital.com/en/numero-01/other-issues/impact-of-climate-change-on-natural-disaster-insurance-in-france

9. World Bank, *A 360 Degree Look at Dominica post Hurricane Maria*. Washington, DC: International Bank for Reconstruction and Development (IBRD) and International Development Association (IDA), 2017. Available from: https://www.worldbank.org/en/news/feature/2017/11/28/a-360-degree-look-at-dominica-post-hurricane-maria

10. I. Anthony, Chief Executive Officer CCRIF SPC, quoted in Herrera, C., "Risk Insurance Builds Climate and Disaster Resilience in Central America and the Caribbean." World Bank, April 21, 2022. Available from: https://www.worldbank.org/en/results/2022/04/21/risk-insurance-builds-climate-and-disaster-resilience-in-central-america-and-the-caribbean

11. Dempsey, B., Hillier, D., *A Dangerous Delay: The Cost of Late Response to Early Warnings in the 2011 Drought in the Horn of Africa*. Inter-Agency Briefing Paper. London: Save the Children and Oxfam, 2012. Available from: https://policy-practice.oxfam.org/resources/a-dangerous-delay-the-cost-of-late-response-to-early-warnings-in-the-2011-droug-203389/

12. Talbot, T., Dercon, S., Barder, O., *Payouts for Perils: How Insurance Can Radically Improve Emergency Aid*. Washington, DC: Center for Global Development, 2017. Available from: www.cgdev.org/node/312519

13. A large pool makes insurance more affordable for each individual country because of diversification; as disasters are unlikely to affect all countries at the same time, reinsurers can spread their risk of a loss across the entire portfolio and so provide their capital at a lower price.

14. CCRIF, *Annual Report 2020–21*. Cayman Islands: CCRIF SPC, 2021 Available from: https://www.ccrif.org/publications/annual-report/ccrif-spc-annual-report-2020-2021?language_content_entity=en

15. CCRIF, "CCRIF Completes Payments Totaling US$29 Million to Member Governments Affected by Hurricane Matthew." October 20, 2016. Available from: https://www.ccrif.org/es/node/11867?page=4

16. Fligstein, N., "Markets as Politics: A Political-Cultural Approach to Market Institutions." *American Sociological Review*, 61(4) (1996): 656–73. https://doi.org/10.2307/2096398

17. Hofstede, G., *Culture's Consequences: Comparing Values, Behaviors, Institutions and Organizations across Nations*. Thousand Oaks, CA: Sage Publications, 2001.

18. Lehtonen, Liukko, "Forms and Limits" "Producing Solidarity."

4

Problem solved?

Between static remits and evolving environments

Introductory Case

Evolving gaps in terrorism insurance. On Saturday June 3, 2017 at around 10 pm, a terrorist attack unfolded on London Bridge. The bridge is a popular tourist destination, just minutes' walk from The Shard and the famous Borough Market. As it was a weekend, the area was busy. In the span of eight minutes, eight people were killed and 48 wounded by terrorists who drove a van at pedestrians and then stabbed multiple people. The terrorists were subsequently shot dead by police.[1]

Borough Market closed for 11 days afterward. Around 100 small businesses, unable to open during this time, suffered combined losses estimated at £1.5 million (~US $1.9 million), with some traders projecting individual losses of up to £30,000 (~US $38,400).[2] There was also a decline in foot traffic in the weeks after the reopening, as people continued to avoid the area.

These losses were significant for such small businesses. They looked to their insurance companies for relief. Business interruption insurance covers organizations for the loss of income caused by a disaster.[3] But Borough Market business owners quickly realized that, if they did have such insurance cover, it only covered business interruption deriving from physical damage to their business premises. No such damage had been caused. This meant traders struggled "to squeeze payouts from insurance companies because of gaps in the way terrorism cover works."[4] The issue was the nature of terrorism insurance policies, rather than any effort by the insurance industry to avoid payment.

Public attention to the plight of the stallholders was high, as was their support. Donations to the Borough Market Traders Relief Fund of around £140,000 (~US $179,200) were made in the month following the attack.[5] Stallholders remarked on the contrast: "when you see the outpouring of generosity from the public, for insurers to shut the door shows they don't

Disaster Insurance Reimagined. Paula Jarzabkowski et al., Oxford University Press. © Paula Jarzabkowski, Konstantinos Chalkias, Eugenia Cacciatori, and Rebecca Bednarek (2023). DOI: 10.1093/oso/9780192865168.003.0004

have any corporate or social responsibility and they don't care about their customers. They should be ashamed of themselves."[6]

As traders ruminated on their lack of protection, there was reputational fallout for the insurance industry: "they [insurers] keep finding loopholes" to avoid "pay[ing] up"[7] As public concern over the problem gained momentum, some MPs began to champion for terrorism insurance cover to support these businesses. Yet advocates for such cover could not turn to the existing terrorism PGE, Pool Re. Its remit, established in the wake of terrorism bombings in the early 1990s causing massive property damage in the UK, did not cover non-damage business interruption.[8] Some people wondered, what was the point in a terrorism insurance pool, and the billions of pounds it had accumulated in its fund, if it did not enable terrorism insurance in the form in which it was most needed?

4.1 Introduction

How do PGEs evolve? Governments establish PGEs when a set of circumstances leads to a specific aspect of uninsurability becoming salient to society. This was the case, for instance, with the withdrawal of terrorism insurance to businesses following the 9/11 terrorist attacks. The solutions brought about by a PGE produce a new equilibrium but tend to be partial, rarely addressing all aspects of uninsurability. In addition, the disasters that PGEs face, and society's expectations of how they should address those disasters, change. A PGE needs to evolve in response both to the *changing nature of its protection gap*, as demonstrated by the terrorist attack that interrupted trading but did not cause property damage, and to the *changing expectations for protection*, such as those of the stallholders and their MPs.

Yet evolution is challenging for PGEs. Their remit is often enshrined in law, or at least solidified and widely understood in custom and practice. This remit establishes the boundaries of what a PGE can do, often narrowly, and those boundaries are usually difficult to change. Further, even when stakeholders agree a PGE should evolve to address new protection gaps, the best way to address a gap is often unclear. For example, the necessary insurance products may not have been developed yet. And stakeholders' interests and expectations about that evolution vary, or even clash, according to their economic, political, and social circumstances.

In this chapter, first, we explore the sources of tensions inherent in PGE evolution. Second, we describe how PGEs navigate those tensions via two different evolutionary patterns. We conclude by providing practical insight into how PGEs can do this difficult yet vital evolutionary work, to remain relevant in the face of the changing nature of risk and expectations for disaster protection.

4.2 Sources of tension in PGE evolution

Efforts to evolve PGEs are often partial, delayed, or even thwarted. This messiness is the result of tensions that PGEs face in three key areas: gaining *recognition* of a mismatch between its current remit and the aspects of uninsurability that are, or soon will be, salient to society; taking the change necessary to address this gap through its *control systems*; and ensuring the change in the remit meets *stakeholder expectations*.

4.2.1 Recognition

PGE managers often recognize and anticipate the shortcomings of the PGE's remit for securing protection from disaster. For example, before the London Bridge attack, Pool Re managers had observed similar attacks overseas and had been raising awareness about the growing need for non-damage business interruption protection. Such gaps in protection may arise because the PGE remit has provided only a partial solution; and/or because the risk is now better understood and more serious than first thought; and/or because the risk itself is changing. Once these additional protection gaps are recognized, PGE managers are then faced with the tension-laden question of whether it is their job to address them.

PGEs are uniquely positioned to recognize or anticipate additional gaps in protection beyond that which they currently provide. This is because they often generate detailed knowledge about a potential disaster and its risk to society. Changes to the risk landscape may not be apparent to other stakeholders, like the government, whose focus is more diffuse. The PGE's role also differs from that of private insurance firms. Insurance companies build detailed knowledge of risk, but any specific insurer's portfolio of risk is commercially confidential information and not shared to build knowledge about an entire population.[9] Further, an insurer's knowledge is often partial and may exclude high-risk parts of the population who are priced out of insurance.[10] By contrast, PGEs often have an implicit or explicit remit to develop knowledge about the risk of a particular disaster to the whole population within a particular region.[11] This role of PGEs in generating, understanding, or collating new and existing knowledge often underpins recognition of a widening protection gap.

Let us consider some examples. First, knowledge generated by PGEs might show that the nature of the disaster has changed. With terrorism, for example, the means of terrorist attacks is continuously shifting.[12] PGEs such as the Australian Reinsurance Pool Corporation (ARPC) have conducted research into the potential for cyber-terrorist attacks.[13] Cyber-attack is an evolution in the nature of terrorism risk that could cause losses that are neither insurable in the private market nor included in the PGE's original remit.[14] Second, the PGE might uncover new insights into a risk that had always existed, but about which society had only partial knowledge. For example, seismic activity may become better understood because of research initiated by a PGE like California Earthquake Authority (CEA). Improved knowledge can lead to new sections of a population being recognized as at high-risk. Yet the PGE's remit may be inadequate to protect this section of the population, newly identified as high-risk and uninsurable in the private market. In these ways PGE managers can recognize gaps in the insurance protection offered within their existing remit. A PGE's *raison d'être* is to offer meaningful protection. Hence, recognition of potential disequilibrium in the insurance landscape is a source of tension for them.

4.2.2 Control systems

PGE managers do not have direct control over their organization's remit. Rather, they are embedded within control systems that legislate, or at least approve, the work that they should undertake. These control systems can take many forms, from public-private governance boards (e.g., Consorcio), to oversight by specific government ministries (e.g., TRIA), to collaborative governance arrangements (e.g., CCRIF, ARC). Such systems are typically embedded within the control paradox, in terms of the extent to which the PGE's role is to enable government or industry control of the insurance market (see Chapters 1 and 3). PGEs must then acquire support from this "control system"—its industry and government stakeholders—to evolve.

Both government and insurance industry tend to need a great deal of convincing that a newly recognized gap *should be* insured, and *cannot* be insured, at least not in full, in the private sector. As one insurer pointed out, they tend to be concerned about "remit creep": "because the PGE exists, it's convenient to ask it to do all this other stuff" (Interview—Insurance Industry). Furthermore, government approval and even legislative change are often required to change a PGE's remit. The control systems around PGEs thus comprise an important set of checks and balances to PGE evolution, aiming to ensure sufficient protection through the PGE without expanding it unnecessarily. As one PGE manager reflected: "the tension that exists is a positive tension because it means we're constantly pushing to do more"

(Interview—PGE). Nonetheless, these tensions must be navigated within the more government- or industry-oriented control system in which any particular PGE is embedded, and can be constraining.

4.2.3 Stakeholder expectations

Government departments and insurance companies are not the only stakeholders that need to be satisfied. Tensions arise when stakeholders' expectations for protection are not met. That is, when the gap between the PGE's remit and the protection offered becomes a problem for some part of the population, such as the small businesses in Borough Market and their MPs.

These stakeholders are often disengaged or unaware of protection gaps unless they personally experience a problem. Insurance, whether delivered by the private sector or by a PGE, is largely a hidden engine of the economy,[15] not noticed except when it is needed or is not working. Thus, a gap in protection might only become salient to these stakeholders when they experience a disaster—as occurred with the Borough Market stallholders. When wider stakeholders *do* become aware of a gap in protection, typically after a disaster, their expectations can change rapidly. The public nature of their loss and their urgent, vocal demands for a solution can put pressure on the government or the insurance industry to act. Heightened stakeholder expectations necessitate a response from the control system[16] and can motivate it to support PGE evolution.

Tensions over stakeholder expectations for protection can thus be a stimulus for change in a PGE's remit. PGE managers can pay attention to stakeholder concerns and use their knowledge of the gap to amplify stakeholder voices, positioning the PGE as a solution. Or in the face of such expectations, a government may turn to an existing PGE, expanding its remit to fulfill the demands upon the government to protect their citizens. For example, in the cases of cyclone-induced flooding in Australia or raging wildfires in California, the insurance industry was unable to provide meaningful protection for a growing area of disaster risk. Like the Borough Market traders' plight, the recurring Australian and Californian disasters raised a groundswell of support for increased protection. Governments cannot force an insurance company to take on more risk. But they can change a PGE's remit. As stakeholder pressure mounted in the context of repeated disasters, the respective governments turned to existing PGEs, expanding the ARPC's remit in Australia to cyclone in 2022 and the CEA's remit in California to wildfire in 2021.

4.3 Parameters that shape evolutionary patterns

To evolve their remit, PGEs must navigate tensions associated with their recognition of a gap, with their control systems, and with stakeholder expectations. The course they steer is shaped by two key parameters, as depicted in Figure 4.1:

1. The perceived urgency to address the recognized gap in protection (vertical axis).
2. The extent to which control over the market is oriented toward the government or the insurance industry (horizontal axis);

Urgency is critical in enabling evolution. Our opening vignette in this chapter described how, before the London Bridge attack, despite recognition by Pool Re, there was little awareness amongst other stakeholders about the gap in protection for terrorism-triggered non-damage business interruption (NDBI). To stimulate change, PGEs need to use their unique knowledge and connections to raise awareness of a protection gap that they

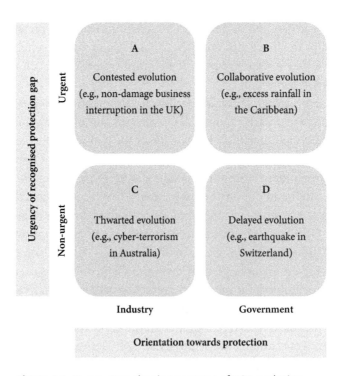

Figure 4.1 Parameters shaping patterns of PGE evolution.

have recognized. A sense of urgency can be built by emphasizing the potential magnitude of impending disaster and/or the time-sensitivity of addressing it. However, all too often, it is only when disaster strikes that heightened awareness of the protection gap decisively increases the urgency to find a solution.

The way a PGE evolves is shaped by the extent to which control over the insurance market is oriented more toward the insurance industry or the government. In some contexts, PGEs are primarily intended to enable the insurance industry to function (as discussed in Chapter 3). Their remit is often designed around leaving insurance protection up to the industry as much as possible. Efforts toward change are usually viewed by both government and the insurance industry as remit creep by PGEs into spaces the private sector could address, as one Treasury official argued: "any time the government intervenes in any way, shape or form … it's a bailout to the industry, which doesn't need it" (Interview—Government). By contrast, in contexts where government control is more prevalent (see Chapter 3), PGEs are intended to provide a widespread societal protection net. Such PGEs typically already have a comprehensive remit and are expected to evolve to meet future challenges. The control system thus throws up fewer barriers to evolution, even if the question of *how* to evolve still presents tensions. Thus, a PGE is embedded in a context of government or industry control that shapes the extent to which it is expected and enabled to evolve.

Taken together these parameters shape four key patterns in attempts to evolve a PGE remit: contested, collaborative, thwarted, and delayed—as shown in Figure 4.1. Those recognized gaps which lack urgency typically mean change is thwarted or, at best, delayed. We, therefore, focus on examining the two urgent evolutionary patterns, which we term contested evolution (Figure 4.1A) and collaborative evolution (Figure 4.1B).

4.4 Contested evolution: Working at the market-edge of disequilibrium

A contested evolution pattern occurs in contexts where industry control over the market is dominant. To limit government intervention, the remit of PGEs in such contexts is typically narrowly defined around a specific aspect of a specific risk. The default position is to contain PGE evolution and avoid "remit creep." In such cases, efforts at evolving to address a gap recognized by PGE managers are typically contested.

4.4.1 Evolving to address non-damage business interruption (NDBI).

We illustrate these dynamics by examining how Pool Re managers worked to expand its remit to cover non-damage business interruption (NDBI) for terrorist attacks. Following the IRA bombing of the Baltic Exchange, Pool Re was established in 1993 to cover the gap in fire- and explosion-based terrorism insurance for commercial property, primarily in the City of London. It has changed a lot since then. For example, following the 2001 World Trade Center attack, Pool Re's remit expanded to include chemical, biological, radiological, and nuclear (CBRN) terrorist attacks. More recently, Pool Re has positioned itself at the forefront of knowledge development on terrorism risk, sponsoring research at universities and employing in-house security experts. In this way, Pool Re has become a leader in recognizing many emerging protection gaps in relation to terrorism risk. Indeed, they had already recognized the gap in NDBI and made government and other stakeholders aware of this, as one participant explained:

> If we look at what happened in Paris [2015] where there was a bunch of marauding gunmen who went and murdered people, well they didn't necessarily cause a huge amount of property damage. What they did cause was a huge amount of non-damage business interruption and they also caused a huge amount of impact on life. So, what we have is a disconnect between the intentions of [terrorism insurance in the UK] and the way that [insurance] policies are responding in the event of a claim.
>
> **(Interview—Government)**

However, acting on this recognized gap was problematic because: "an expansion of the remit requires a new Act of Parliament, new legislation" (Interview—PGE). As often happens, it took a disaster—the London Bridge terrorist attack—to stimulate evolution. As explained in the opening vignette, the 2017 London Bridge terrorist attack meant many small businesses had to close temporarily. As their properties suffered no physical damage, they did not have insurance for their losses: "non-damage business interruption was not covered because nobody had thought of it before. They'd thought that there would always be a bomb and so you would never have non-damage business interruption" (Interview—PGE). In short, terrorism as a risk was evolving to encompass a much wider threat than Pool Re's focus on property damage.

While Pool Re had recognized a gap in NDBI protection prior to the attack, they had initially struggled to raise urgency for any change. Yet they continued to generate knowledge, expanding their stakeholder network to include the Office for Security and Counter Terrorism (OSCT), and to provoke the attention of a wider group of stakeholders around the necessity of NDBI protection.

Following the London Bridge attack, as extended closure caused small businesses to lose both customers and perishable goods, Pool Re drew on the knowledge it had amassed. It moved quickly to champion these stakeholders, whose expectation for protection became urgent as they experienced losses. Empathizing with the stallholders, Pool Re bemoaned the fact that NDBI was outside their remit. Media attention focused on the effects of non-insurance for small businesses, helping to raise awareness about the limitations of the Pool Re remit. For example, the *Financial Times* noted that: "Pool Re, the government-backed terrorism insurer, was set up by the government of the day in the early 1990s to provide cover after IRA bombings in the City of London. But it is only allowed to pay out if the claimant has suffered property damage."[17]

The government was aware that the relatively small losses were within the reach of the private insurance industry. As an official argued: "if you max-out the modeling for non-damage business interruption, individual insurers can still pay for it" (Interview—Government). Pool Re pointed out that: "NDBI is something that the insurance industry—if they had a will and if they thought there was a sufficient profit incentive—could fill themselves" (Interview—PGE). There were thus growing stakeholder expectations, within government and the business community, that the private sector should offer protection from NDBI. And all the while, Pool Re continued to use its specialist knowledge to raise awareness about the potential scale of the risk. As one participant commented on some analysis that Pool Re had provided:

Non-damage business interruption for businesses during an active shooter event in a city which is deliberately locked down by the security forces. Say if every single business in London is shut down for three days? The entire market doesn't want to carry that risk because it's too much.

(Interview—Government)

Urgency was built, but of course the government could not *force* an insurance industry response. The cost and effort to develop such a product at speed was not a high priority for the private sector, given the modest returns. As one insurer admitted, "the private sector in the UK ain't going to do it until it has its arse kicked by somebody" (Interview—Insurance Industry).

Under reputational pressure for a solution, and yet without products at hand, the insurance industry began to point to Pool Re as a possible solution. "Almost without exception, they said no. We don't want to do that [terrorism NDBI]. We don't understand it. We can't model it. We want Pool Re to do it" (Interview—PGE). The professional body, the Association of British Insurers, proposed that "to help insurers support businesses, Pool Re's function could be extended to cover business interruption."[18] Some MPs joined in on these suggestions.

Pool Re was thus seen by all stakeholders as being able to provide a timely solution to address the recognized gap. They would use their modeling to develop a product with the aim that it would eventually revert to the private sector once established: "trying to get the industry to expand cover … it was going to take ten/fifteen years at least. So, we have got a mechanism that accelerates the privatization of terrorism risk" (Interview—PGE).

The process, while initially contested, reached a point of urgency at which both government's fundamental reluctance to intervene and the private market's antagonism toward remit creep were overcome. The required legislative change was achieved in 2018:

> When businesses raised their concerns about a gap in insurance cover following a terror attack, we worked with Pool Re to come up with a solution. Today, we've changed the law to give businesses peace of mind, helping them to insure themselves against financial loss as a result of a terrorist attack, even if there is no physical damage to their property.[19]

As the amendment to their remit was passed, Pool Re's CEO noted: "our priority has been to keep this as far as possible a private market solution."[20] The product was launched with the expectation that it could soon be offered within the private sector.

4.4.2 From contested to thwarted evolution

In a context that considers insurance industry control over the market as the best way to achieve protection for society, PGE evolution is often thwarted. With the NDBI extension of its remit, Pool Re had generated the grounds for a wider role. It had positioned itself as capable of recognizing gaps in protection and informing society about—and questioning—looming disequilibrium: "we want to take the opportunity [building from success in changing NDBI] to … adapt the Pool Re scheme to meet whatever manifestations of the terrorism threat were causing uninsured loss and damage (Interview—PGE).

Yet, despite these efforts to expand the PGE remit, Pool Re's provision of cover for terrorism NDBI remained modest, as the immediate threat of such terrorist attacks subsided. Small businesses owners no longer experienced urgency to address this threat. Yet the government was reluctant to intervene with any mandatory insurance scheme. Rather, the 2022 five-yearly government review of Pool Re recommended a reduction in pricing and an awareness campaign to help small businesses recognize the benefits of terrorism cover. The contested process of PGE evolution continued.

4.5 Collaborative evolution: Making the collective work for the individuals

Case 4.1 is an example of a collaborative evolutionary pattern (see Figure 4.1B). The collaborative pattern is prevalent in those PGEs that take a government-led approach toward the benefits that insurance should provide (see Chapter 1). Multi-country risk pools, such as ARC and CCRIF, are particularly strong examples of the collaborative approach because they need to balance both elements of the control system carefully. They need insurance industry capital to provide for losses. Yet their purpose is not to provide profits for the insurance industry, but to ensure that the insurance market can provide benefits to their government members. In these contexts, control systems behave in very different ways to those seen in contested patterns. The PGE is expected to evolve to address societal needs for protection and needs to work *with* a diffuse control system comprising governments, the insurance industry, and wider stakeholders in achieving social aims for protection.

Case example 4.1: Collaborative evolution in the African Risk Capacity.

The African Risk Capacity (ARC) is a multi-country PGE, established in 2012 to provide drought insurance products to African countries. ARC needs a critical mass of countries to form a big enough pool to enable it to buy cost-effective insurance policies from international reinsurance markets for its member countries. A large pool makes insurance more affordable for each individual country because of diversification; as disasters are unlikely to affect all countries at the same time, reinsurers can spread their risk of a loss across the entire portfolio and, so, provide their capital at a lower price.[a]

Throughout the early years of its existence ARC struggled. It managed to keep only 4-6 countries in the pool; too few to comprise a collective basis for protection[b] and ARC was engaged in "ongoing efforts to ensure more countries sign up to support this mechanism."[c]

ARC managers thus needed to work at bringing on board new members. They did so by expanding their remit collaboratively through a range of initiatives. First, in collaboration with countries, they expanded from crop drought to also cover grazing-range drought and tropical cyclone to better meet countries' varied needs for protection. Second, in collaboration with donors, they introduced donor-subsidized financing of premiums for some countries, enabling them to join the pool or to retain them in the pool during a period of economic hardship. Third, in collaboration with donors and humanitarian organizations, they introduced new humanitarian members, such as Start Network and the World Food Program. While not country members, these organizations increased the size of the pool by purchasing products to enable them to meet their humanitarian objectives for disaster relief within different ARC countries.

Via this collaborative process with a wide range of stakeholders, ARC was able to grow the collective pool.[d] By 2022 they had 24 members across a range of products, a mix of humanitarian and country members, and a variety of subsidized and country-paid premiums. This expansion of their remit in terms of their initial product (crop drought) and members (governments) enabled ARC to meet its overarching social remit to "help African governments improve their capacities to better plan, prepare, and respond to extreme weather events and natural disasters."[e] The evolution had not been easy. Multiple different donors from countries around the world had to be brought on board, even as different countries moved in and out of the pool for a range of reasons including changes in government, loss of confidence in insurance, or lack of resources. Further, the need for evolution is ongoing. Despite a more robust pool by 2022, ARC managers knew they needed to continue to work hard at developing the collective pooling mechanism to ensure protection for their individual members.

[a] Christophers, B., Bigger, P., Johnson, L., "Stretching Scales? Risk and Sociality in Climate Finance." *Environment and Planning A: Economy and Space*, 52(1) (2020): 88–110. https://doi.org/10.1177/0308518X18819004
[b] Johnson, L., "Rescaling Index Insurance for Climate and Development in Africa." *Economy and Society*, 50(2) (2021): 248–74. https://doi.org/10.1080/03085147.2020.1853364. Linnerooth-Bayer, J., Mechler, R., "Disaster Safety Nets for Developing Countries: Extending Public–Private Partnerships." *Environmental Hazards*, 7(1) (2007): 54–61. https://doi.org/10.1016/j.envhaz.2007.04.004
[c] "ARC Member States." Date accessed: September 2022. Available from: https://www.arc.int/countries
[d] "ARC Member States." Johnson, "Rescaling Index Insurance."
[e] ARC, "About the African Risk Capacity Group." Date accessed: September 2022. Available from: https://www.arc.int

Even though this control system is not intended to curtail PGE evolution, it often remains unclear how the PGE should best evolve. For example, there may not be products to address the recognized gaps, and stakeholders may be uncertain about whether proposed solutions will address their problems.[21] Furthermore, if countries do not feel that the PGE is providing adequate protection and value for them, they can easily leave the pool. Therefore, managers in these PGEs need to work collaboratively, engaging with multiple stakeholders to enable evolution.

We now explore this collaborative pattern in more detail focusing on CCRIF, a multi-country risk pool made up of 22 member countries. As with the contested pattern, typically the occurrence of a disaster triggers the evolution process. Disasters highlight gaps, provide an impetus to develop more knowledge about them, and provide a specific focus for improving protection.[22] Disasters can often be the difference between delayed evolution and building enough urgency for stakeholders to collaborate on change. Our story of CCRIF's evolution, therefore, revolves around such a disaster.

4.5.1 Evolving to develop new products for protection

CCRIF's remit is explicitly focused on working with member countries to recognize their various disaster liquidity needs and prepare for them physically and financially.[23] It is supposed to help develop knowledge about disasters within the region and build members' understanding of them. Given these expectations, CCRIF's history has been one of continuous collaborative evolution. We now illustrate this process through the example of the aftermath of Hurricane "Harper."[24]

Disasters like Hurricane Harper expose inconsistencies in the collective system of a multi-country risk pool, in terms of which countries did or did not get a payout. After Hurricane Harper swept through the region, some countries sustained higher levels of damage but, because of the amount of insurance cover they had purchased, received lower payments. While the variation in payments was consistent with the insurance contracts purchased, pool members were dissatisfied: "but the losses in Country B were not as devastating as what was seen in Country A. So, there was this discrepancy, people trying to understand how can you pay out more for a government like Country B?" (Interview—Development Agency). The accompanying outrage exposed unmet expectations for protection on the part of the member countries: "you're bleeding money to pay for these products which you don't see how they are addressing any of your vulnerability needs. So where is it going?" (Interview—Government). These experiences were not uniform. Indeed, some countries had positive experiences from the payments they received. One explained that "within one week we received the money. The President declared a state of emergency and we can use the money to respond" (Interview—Government).

The varied experiences of the countries helped the PGE recognize gaps in the cover offered and in stakeholders' expectations for protection. At any point, a country member of CCRIF can decide their individual needs are not being adequately met within the collective pool and withdraw from it. If CCRIF could not get stakeholder expectations to match the protection they could offer, they would be unable to retain sufficient members and potentially fail as a solution. PGE managers sprang into action. They worked individually and directly with countries, modeling the outcomes from the disaster to understand both why countries felt their needs had not been addressed, and what might be done to improve the protection that could be offered. This helped them understand stakeholder expectations and collaborate with them on the ongoing evolution of protection.

One such evolution was the development of an excess rainfall product. Some countries found that the hurricane products they had purchased were not triggered by Hurricane Harper. This was because the damage it caused was not related to wind speed (the usual focus of a hurricane product) but excess rainfall (which is extremely heavy rainfall over a concentrated period). The PGE and its stakeholders recognized a protection gap for excess rainfall—a risk for which no insurance product already existed for governments in that region.

To develop such a product, PGE managers collaborated with their range of stakeholders. They worked with meteorologists and modeling companies, building the knowledge to develop this new product, and with the reinsurance industry to ensure their confidence to underwrite the product with industry capital.[25] But the collaboration reached far wider: they also approached donors and development organizations to mobilize their support for a roll-out of the new product across the Caribbean.[26] They collaborated on testing the potential viability of the products—both for the countries involved and for the private-sector insurers. Any new product had to be something that multiple countries would be willing to buy, to strengthen CCRIF's collective system, and also be appropriately priced to attract private-sector capital to underwrite the risk. As one insurer stated: "I do get the social thing. But at the same time, we're publicly listed companies, we are not charities. We have shareholders, so we have to charge an appropriate premium" (Interview—Insurance Industry).

This collaborative process was important for CCRIF's evolution because of the diffuse nature of the control system in such contexts. As the product was launched, the President of the Caribbean Development Bank, Dr. Warren Smith, emphasized that collaboration among CCRIF, donors, and regional organizations was "enhancing the disaster-risk management capacity of the region as a whole."[27] This example of the collaborative pattern shows how, even when a PGE places government members' needs for protection at the heart of its remit, the process of evolution is enormously complex. PGEs like CCRIF evolve incrementally as gaps in protection are recognized and, over time, incorporated into a collaborative approach to protection. The basis for this ongoing change is an assumption that the PGE *should* change to address new sources of disequilibrium. Any specific disaster may feel like a point of imminent disequilibrium, in which the whole system of protection could break down. However, the collaborative pattern holds that disequilibrium at bay, as the solution itself emerges within the collaborations between stakeholders and the PGE.

4.5.2 From collaborative to delayed

The complexity of the collaborative process, necessitating interactions amongst multiple stakeholders, means that any evolution of the remit can also be delayed. Even though there is an assumption that a PGE will evolve to address gaps in protection, a sense of urgency is still needed to provide impetus to this complex process.

The Swiss system provides an example of how, despite its strong orientation toward government control of the market for the benefit of society, PGE evolution can be delayed. The Swiss system of disaster insurance is comprehensive. The exception to this is earthquake disaster risk, which was not included in the early set-up of the system. The existence of this significant protection gap has been recognized for decades. However, the Swiss system, which includes highly regulated market provision in some cantons, and PGEs in the form of cantonal public sector insurers in others (see Chapter 5), has struggled to evolve to include earthquake cover. In contrast to the tension in a contested evolution, the PGEs and the insurance industry agreed that earthquakes would be best covered within the existing disaster insurance system rather than by pure private-sector provision. However, tensions persist and have delayed evolution. These tensions derive from the perception that the current bundle of risks is good value for money and balanced in terms of cost and benefits across cantons. However, earthquake risk is very unevenly distributed, with some cantons highly exposed and some far less so.[28] The cantonal government stakeholders and individual policyhold-ers within less risk-exposed areas pushed back on evolving the PGE remit to include earthquake cover; "as we are a federal country with 26 cantons, with 26 opinions, we did not succeed to get it ... too many cantons said no, we don't want that" (Interview—Insurance Industry).

The cantonal PGEs and the insurance industry continued to collaborate on raising awareness about the gap and developed schemes through which cover could easily be provided within the existing system: "the solution, even the price, it was very, very affordable" (Interview—Insurance Indus-try). However, the lack of support of some key stakeholders has meant that these initiatives have yet to bear fruit.[29] Both industry and PGEs believe that their efforts to raise awareness and expand their remit are delayed rather than thwarted. They expect that a disaster will build the urgency that has so far been lacking and that will shift stakeholders' expectations: "I think the more we get little earthquakes, ... the more it gets into the heads of the people ... OK, this is really necessary to have" (Interview—Insurance Industry). Yet, as this example shows, even within a government-oriented approach to pro-tection, the evolution of a PGE's remit is always tension-laden and may be delayed when a sense of urgency is missing.

4.6 Conclusion: PGE evolution is vital to keep pace with the changing nature of disaster

Evolution is vital for PGEs, as insurance protection gaps and the understand-ing of them change over time—sometimes dramatically. If they cannot evolve around newly recognized gaps, PGEs run the risk of becoming less relevant in their role of enabling protection that cannot be provided within the pri-vate sector. This chapter has shown how an orientation toward industry or government control over protection, together with the urgency of the recog-nized gap, shapes different patterns of evolution (see Figure 4.1). PGEs use that urgency to expose the potential disequilibrium of unprotected risk as a basis to evolve. Our chapter shows that evolution is vital but hard-won via two main patterns: contested and collaborative.

To enable change through contested or collaborative evolution, PGE man-agers need to address three key tensions associated with evolution: raising awareness of recognized gaps (Figure 4.2A), acting through the control sys-tem (Figure 4.2B), and addressing stakeholder expectations (Figure 4.2C). Evolution involves a process of interaction with the control system and wider

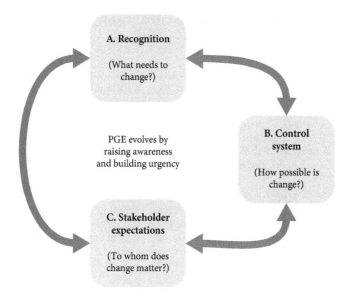

Figure 4.2 A framework for PGE evolution.

stakeholders to raise awareness of a recognized impending disequilibrium in the insurance system and build urgency to address it; ideally before a disaster makes the associated uninsurability an immense problem for unprotected sections of society. These sources of variation and the different patterns of navigating the three key tensions via which PGEs evolve are summarized in Table 4.1.

In this chapter, we highlighted the difficulties of PGE evolution. People often think that "good" change is a smooth process, but those working in the protection gap space should have different expectations. PGE change is often triggered by disasters that reveal unmet stakeholder expectations. As stakeholders grapple with physical, financial, social, and emotional hardship after disasters, their expectations for protection are always going to be fraught with tensions. PGE evolution often occurs at this point of dissatisfaction with existing solutions, which typically also highlights a gap in the protection provided by the PGE: for example, stakeholders finding out that Pool Re did not cover business interruption, or countries realizing that the existing CCRIF hurricane product did not meet their needs for protection from extreme rainfall. The reality is that no PGE can be the perfect solution, nor can societies ever be protected fully from disaster losses. But this dissatisfaction—and yes, pain—can at least be used as an engine of change. We hope that this can be an enabling perspective given the realities of working within the protection gap space.

Table 4.1 An overarching framework to explain PGE evolution

	Contested Pattern (Industry-control-oriented)	Collaborative pattern (Government-control-oriented)
A. Recognized protection gap	PGE uses knowledge to recognize and raise awareness about the gap relevant to their domain	
	The PGE's remit may involve developing knowledge of new protection gaps but not evolving to address those gaps.	The PGE's remit is generally assumed to involve developing the knowledge to recognize gaps AND evolving to address them.
	Disasters: Increase recognition of, and insight into, protection gaps.	
B. Control System	Protection in the form of insurance is assumed to be best provided by the insurance industry. There are widespread fears of remit creep and the control systems' default is to stop PGE evolution. Legislative change is required for any change beyond a *narrowly defined* existing remit.	Protection via insurance is controlled by the government on behalf of its citizens. The PGE's remit to offer protection is *comprehensive* rather than narrow. Hence, the system is open to PGE evolution, albeit the best way to evolve may still need considerable negotiation.
	Disasters: help build urgency that makes the control system more likely to enable PGE evolution rather than thwart or delay it.	
C. Stakeholder expectations	Salience of the protection gap for different stakeholders fluctuates; stakeholders can be oblivious to or highly conscious of the gap. PGEs can work to raise awareness and thus expectations for change.	
	Stakeholders assume protection is provided by the insurance industry. They tend to be unaware of recognized gaps until they are made salient by a disaster. Post-disaster expectations for protection become urgent and may trigger the control system to expand the PGE remit to address that protection.	Stakeholders expect the government to ensure that the insurance market provides adequate protection from disasters. They tend to be unaware of recognized gaps until they are made salient by a disaster. Post-disaster, they are likely to express an urgent need for expanded protection and to assume that a PGE will evolve to provide this protection.
	Disasters clarify and increase stakeholder expectations for protection and build urgency for PGE evolution	

4.6.1 Looking ahead: Potentially the most meaningful evolution of all

We end this chapter with a final point regarding *the direction* in which PGEs might evolve. As the potential for disaster increases, PGEs can play a key role in avoiding disequilibrium by evolving to enhance society's resilience to these disasters. They need to move beyond just offering financial protection post-disaster to helping society to avert the effects of disasters. For example, as flooding increases due to climate change, it becomes essential to build more physical resilience to that risk, such as changing how we build and even relocating at-risk communities. Chapter 5 explores the complex question of the role that PGEs can play in the physical resilience of societies as part of their ongoing evolution.

4.7 Learning points

1. Focusing on recognizing protection gaps. Building the knowledge necessary to recognize protection gaps is a critical role for PGEs, regardless of their ability to directly address those gaps. This knowledge can be used to either prompt other stakeholders to address recognized gaps or enable the PGE to act quickly after a disaster creates the urgency to find a solution. The ability to recognize gaps is thus an important PGE achievement in its own right.

2. Building urgency and awareness (pre-disaster). Raising awareness and building urgency about impending disequilibrium is a critical role for PGEs, as societies can sleep-walk toward even foreseeable disasters,[30] such as the climate crisis. Disasters are typically a key stimulus for building urgency (see Table 4.1). As a next step PGEs can, however, use our framework to consider how they could raise awareness and build urgency to increase protection prior to disasters.

3. Relationships. Evolution for PGEs is always relational.[31] Whether collaborative or contested, evolution involves repeated interactions with multiple stakeholders over time. PGEs can use our framework to distinguish between stakeholders who form their control system and the wider stakeholders whose expectations for protection can impact that control system. They could then identify how their relationships with these groups, and the interactions between the groups, constrain and enable their evolutionary process. Despite the challenges to evolution, we regard this web of relationships as a largely positive system of checks and balances—one that ensures PGEs pay attention to stakeholders and their most pressing needs for protection.

4. Stakeholder engagement. Our findings also have implications for the stakeholders surrounding the PGE, particularly those government and insurance organizations that comprise the main control system. By better understanding the role that PGEs play, particularly in alleviating the

financial hardship of post-disaster response, these stakeholders might also consider how they can better facilitate the evolution of the PGE to meet the demands of a changing disaster landscape. Our work should alert those stakeholders that, while forming checks and balances on PGE evolution is important, so is enabling thoughtful change.

Notes

1. Perraudin, F., "Borough Market Reopens 11 Days after London Bridge Attack." *The Guardian*, June 14, 2017. Available from: https://www.theguardian.com/uk-news/2017/jun/14/borough-market-reopens-london-bridge-attack.

   Osborne, S., "Londona Attack: Death Toll Rises to Eight after Body Believed to be French Tourist Xavier Thomas Recovered from Thames." *Independent*, June 7, 2017. Available from: https://www.independent.co.uk/news/uk/home-news/london-attack-xavier-thomas-body-french-tourist-thames-bridge-river-missing-limehouse-met-police-borough-market-a7776746.html

2. Casciani, D., "Terror Attacks: Closing Legal Loophole will Give Firms Insurance Cover." *BBC News*, February 12, 2019. Available from: https://www.bbc.co.uk/news/uk-47217649.

   Bourke, J., "Borough Market Traders Hit with Losses after London Bridge Attack Ask Government for Financial Help." *Evening Standard*, July 18, 2017. Available from: https://www.standard.co.uk/news/london/borough-market-traders-hit-with-losses-in-wake-of-london-bridge-terror-attack-ask-government-for-financial-help-a3590236.html

3. Harrington, J. S., Dudey, P. O., *Questions about Business Income Insurance*. Issue 3057. New York: Adjusting Today, 2021. Available from: https://www.adjustersinternational.com/publications/adjusting-today/questions-about-business-income-insurance

4. Pickard, J., Ralph, O., "Insurers Urged to Widen UK Terror Cover after London Attacks." *Financial Times*, July 14, 2017. Available from: https://www.ft.com/content/81f3f0ce-67de-11e7-9a66-93fb352ba1fe

5. Pickard, Ralph, "Insurers Urged."

6. Ralph, O., "Insurers Look to Broaden Policies to Cover Terrorism." *Financial Times*, June 23, 2017. Available from: https://www.ft.com/content/a72e39fc-5740-11e7-9fed-c19e2700005f

7. Cumming, E., "Back in Business: One Month after the Borough Market Attack." *The Guardian*, July 2, 2017. Available from: https://www.theguardian.com/lifeandstyle/2017/jul/02/borough-market-one-month-after-the-terror-attack

8. Ralph, O., Pickard, J., "Terrorism Insurance Costs Cut for Small UK Businesses." *Financial Times*, October 12, 2017. Available from: https://www.ft.com/content/849a25f8-ae99-11e7-beba-5521c713abf4

9. Timms, P. D., Hillier, J. K., Holland, C. P., "Increase Data Sharing or Die? An Initial View for Natural Catastrophe Insurance." *Geography*, 107(1) (2022): 26–37. https://doi.org/10.1080/00167487.2022.2019494

10. Holland, C. P., Zarkadakis, G., Hillier, J., Timms, P. D., Stanbrough, L., "Data Sharing Models in the Insurance Industry." *WTW*, February 22, 2021. Available from: https://www.wtwco.com/en-AU/Insights/2021/02/data-sharing-models-in-the-insurance-industry

11. Nussbaum, R., "Involving Public Private Partnerships as Building Blocks for Integrated Natural Catastrophes Country Risk Management: Sharing on the French National Experiences of Economic Instruments Integrated with Information and Knowledge Management Tools." *IDRiM Journal*, 5(2) (2015): 82–100. https://doi.org/10.5595/idrim.2015.0116.

    See EQC's statuary function to "fund research and education on natural disasters and ways of reducing their impact": https://www.eqc.govt.nz/about-eqc/our-role/.

    Also, CEA, "California Residential Mitigation Program" (CRMP): https://www.californiaresidentialmitigationprogram.com/About-CRMP/CEA-History#:~:text=The%20California%20Earthquake%20Authority%20(CEA,risk%20of%20earthquake%20losses%20through (both accessed September 2022).

12. Cummins, J. D., "Should the Government Provide Insurance for Catastrophes." *Federal Reserve Bank of St. Louis Review*, 88(4) (2006): 337–79.

    Ericson, R., Doyle, A., "Catastrophe Risk, Insurance and Terrorism." *Economy and Society*, 33(2) (2004): 135–73. https://doi.org/10.1080/03085140410001677102

13. OECD, *Insurance Coverage for Cyber Terrorism in Australia*. Paris: OECD, 2020. Available from: https://www.oecd.org/finance/insurance/Insurance-Coverage-for-Cyber-Terrorism-in-Australia.htm

14. Jimeno Muñoz, J., "Cyber risks: Liability and insurance." *InDret*. (2019), 2.

15. Hufeld, F., Koijen, R., Thimann, C., "The Invisible Service: The Economics, Regulation, and Systemic Risk of Insurance Markets." *CEPR*, January 30, 2017. Available from: https://cepr.org/voxeu/columns/invisible-service-economics-regulation-and-systemic-risk-insurance-markets

16. Elliott, R., *Underwater: Loss, Flood Insurance, and the Moral Economy of Climate Change in the United States*. New York: Columbia University Press, 2021.

17. Pickard, Ralph, "Insurers Urged."

18. Pickard, Ralph, "Insurers Urged."

19. Glen, J., quoted in HM Treasury, "Terrorism Insurance Gap Closed Giving Peace of Mind to Businesses." February 12, 2019. Available from: https://www.gov.uk/government/news/terrorism-insurance-gap-closed-giving-peace-of-mind-to-businesses

20. Insurance Journal, "UK's Pool Re Extends Terrorism Cover to Include Non-Damage Business Interruption." February 13, 2019. Available from: https://www.insurancejournal.com/news/international/2019/02/13/517548.htm

21. Elliott, *Underwater*.

    Jarzabkowski, P., Bednarek, R., Chalkias, K., Cacciatori, E., "Exploring Inter-Organizational Paradoxes: Methodological Lessons from a Study of a Grand Challenge." *Strategic Organization*, 17(1) (2019: 120–32. https://doi.org/10.1177/1476127018805345

22. Johnson, L., Wandera, B., Jensen, N., Banerjee, R., "Competing Expectations in an Index-Based Livestock Insurance Project." *Journal of Development Studies*, 55(6) (2019): 1221–39. https://doi.org/10.1080/00220388.2018.1453603

23. CCRIF, "Strategic Objectives." Date accessed: September 2022. Available from: https://www.ccrif.org/aboutus/strategic-objectives

24. To preserve the confidentiality of specific participants, we disguise the name and year of the hurricane and anonymize the names of all countries.

25. CCRIF, Swiss Re, *Excess Rainfall Product: A Guide to Understanding This New Product*. Barbados: CCRIF, October 2012. Available from: https://www.ccrif.org/sites/default/files/publications/ExcessRainfall-Booklet-November2012.pdf

26. CCRIF, *Regional Donors and Organisations Discuss CCRIF's New Excess Rainfall Product*. Cayman Islands: CCRIF, March 15, 2013. Available from: https://www.ccrif.org/node/474?language_content_entity=en

27. CCRIF, *Regional Donors.*

28. Mayoraz, J., Lacave, C., Duvernay, B., *Erdbeben: Karten der baugrundklassen.* Umwelt-Wissen, 1603. Bern: Bundesamt für Umwelt, 2016. Available from: https://www.bafu.admin.ch/bafu/de/home/themen/naturgefahren/publikationen-studien/publikationen/erdbeben-karten-der-baugrundklassen.html

29. Neue Zürcher Zeitung, "Keine versicherung für erdbeben." June 20, 2010. Available from: https://www.nzz.ch/keine_versicherung_fuer_erdbeben-ld.943852.

    Mueller, A., "Durch die pandemie wachgerüttelt? Für hausbesitzer steht eine obligatorische 'erdbebenversicherung light' vor der tür." *Neue Zürcher Zeitung*, September 22, 2021. Available from: https://www.nzz.ch/wirtschaft/erdbeben-versicherung-nach-pandemie-beben-in-bundesbern-ld.1646588

30. Unger, C., *Insidious Risk Management: A Practice Theoretical Perspective*. Brisbane: UQ Business School, University of Queensland, 2021. https://doi.org/10.14264/2393daa

31. Jarzabkowski, P., Bednarek, R., Spee, P., *Making a Market for Acts of God: The Practice of Risk-Trading in the Global Reinsurance Industry*. New York: Oxford University Press, 2015.

5
Limiting loss

Between financial and physical resilience

Introductory Case

The "hot potato" of resilience. We participated in a few conferences in quick succession where the insurance protection gap was discussed by industry, government, and other stakeholders. Resilience was a persistent theme across the separate events. Physical resilience—in the form of better buildings, wiser land use, and improved response—is the answer, insurance industry experts confidently said. Multiple times. Yet it also felt like the insurance industry was treating resilience as a "hot potato"; something to be passed over to other stakeholders as quickly as possible. If the answer was resilience, clearly that was not within the bounds of the insurance industry's responsibility—it is not insurers who set urban planning guidelines or build flood barriers. As we stepped away from these conferences, we were left with a lingering disquiet. By invoking physical resilience, insurance industry stakeholders distanced themselves from the protection gap, enabling them to work from a position where they felt comfortable, leaving their role and practices fundamentally unchanged. Ensuring financial resilience by pricing risk and providing funds to address the consequences of disaster was an insurance role; developing the physical aspect of resilience and building more resilient communities was something for the public sector. Yet we were left wondering how the two could be more deeply and meaningfully connected.

5.1 Introduction

Insurance and resilience have become increasingly connected in discussions of how to deal with the protection gap. Insurance provides financial resilience by delivering sufficient funding for reconstruction after a disaster. Physical resilience addresses the need for properties and people to be less vulnerable to damage from disaster in the first place, through investment in prevention and mitigation. The conference participants shared the

Disaster Insurance Reimagined. Paula Jarzabkowski et al., Oxford University Press. © Paula Jarzabkowski, Konstantinos Chalkias, Eugenia Cacciatori, and Rebecca Bednarek (2023). DOI: 10.1093/oso/9780192865168.003.0005

understanding that, in a context in which disasters are becoming more frequent and severe,[1] physical resilience is crucial to maintaining insurability. Without it the losses—and the premiums—threaten to become unaffordable. But who should take responsibility for improving physical resilience? In this chapter, we explain why answering this question involves reshaping the control and responsibility paradoxes.

Taking responsibility for physical resilience is not a trivial problem. Resilience is not simply a matter of investing in individual properties; it is also generated by flood defenses, planning and building regulations, disaster-response services such as firefighting, and even communications during disasters. A real web of stakeholders! And physical resilience derives not just from these elements in isolation, but from how they interact with each other as a complex system. This means that individual property owners are not the only ones responsible for reducing their risk. That responsibility needs to be shared with other stakeholders, such as environment agencies, planners, legislators, disaster services, the building industry, and, yes, the insurance industry as well. We need to figure out how to identify and coordinate responsibilities between individuals, their immediate communities, and also central and local governments, who are the major players in important issues such as land-use planning and building standards. Effective physical resilience thus involves connecting and coordinating stakeholders outside of the traditional boundaries of the insurance industry. In the face of a complex and widespread threat like the climate crisis, many different stakeholders need to be involved if we are to reduce risk to the point where the various disasters are insurable. These new relationships will involve new dynamics within the responsibility and control paradoxes. PGEs, which straddle the public-private boundary, appear ideally suited to supporting this new equilibrium.

To achieve this, though, a PGE's main priorities must be reversed. Rather than seeing physical resilience as a complement to their role in making risk insurable, they need to see insurance as a complement to their role in making the built environment physically resilient. Only when PGEs operate within these reversed priorities, can new balances in the responsibility and control paradoxes be found from which a new sustainable equilibrium can emerge. With this change in remit, PGEs will be able to make a meaningful impact on long-term insurability of disasters.

We propose this dramatic adjustment in PGEs' focus because making insurance available, the primary objective of most PGEs, can have unintended negative consequences for physical resilience. By increasing financial resilience through the provision of affordable insurance PGEs might end up weakening some of the pricing signals that indicate the need for physical resilience.[2] This is especially the case when affordability is emphasized. For example, as one PGE manager mused:

> Maybe insurance coverage wouldn't be available in some locations if it wasn't for [the PGE]. Because private insurers, they'd be like "no, we'll be out of here, thanks, we're not covering tops of cliff and floodplains and fault zones." So, with [PGE] and the government enabling people to live in these higher-risk areas maybe it is taking away the absolute incentive to adapt and mitigate to climate change effects.
>
> **(Interview—PGE)**

If PGEs mask pricing signals in a world of increasing disaster, they will undermine motivations to increase physical resilience, meaning that losses are likely to grow over time in a way that will, in turn, undermine insurability. Thus, to ensure the availability and affordability of insurance in the long term, PGEs need to give priority to physical resilience, integrating insurance as a tool to achieve it.

The task for PGEs is not simple. Integrating physical and financial resilience involves changing the nature and scope of the PGE's remit. It also involves new webs of relationships with different stakeholders beyond those traditionally involved in insurance. Many PGEs confront the problem that, without these changes, they will have little or no impact on long-term resilience and thus might also end up unable to provide insurance any longer. This chapter reviews possible approaches to resilience and explains how PGEs currently handle the integration of physical and financial resilience. We will show that a fundamental reconfiguration of the responsibility and control paradoxes is necessary if we are to achieve this integration and ensure the ongoing sustainability of insurance.

5.2 Approaches to resilience

Approaches to resilience vary in scope and temporal horizon. They can also be situated along a continuum from "return-to-normal" at one end to "adaptation" at the other.[3] We now explore the tensions in these positions on the continuum.

5.2.1 Tensions in resilience as back-to-normal or adaptation

When resilience is understood as "return-to-normal" the focus is on the specific asset affected (e.g., the specific building), the ability to avoid disturbances to its normal operations (e.g., through measures that avoid water entering the building during a flood), and, failing that, the ability to restore normal operations quickly (e.g., through easily cleanable floors in case of floods). The scope is limited (the specific building), time horizons are relatively short (the floods we can reasonably expect), and the appropriateness of "normal operation" is not questioned (for instance, whether building should be allowed in that location). The emphasis is on restoring the pre-disaster situation as quickly as possible. The danger is that ways to avoid damage in the first place, or reduce it, are missed.

At the other end of the continuum, resilience means "adaptation." Rather than returning to normal, the aim is to reconfigure the whole system to be better prepared for future crises. Here, the scope of the system under consideration extends to include institutional structures, such as where people are expected to live and work, and considerable changes in that system may be undertaken. Further, the time horizon extends to the long term as this approach considers the potential future disequilibrium that anticipated disasters can bring to the insurance system (see Chapter 4).

Based on this contrast, approaches to resilience can be seen as operating across tensions between narrow and broad scope and short- and long-term time horizons,[4] as shown in Figure 5.1.

Further complexities regarding resilience derive from the cyclical nature of disaster management,[5] which takes place across pre-, during-, and post-disaster phases. During a disaster, attention is focused on the system affected and ensuring a rapid and effective response. The urgency of the situation tends to bring a short-term focus: for example, repairing houses quickly to ensure that people can get back into them, albeit at the expense of longer

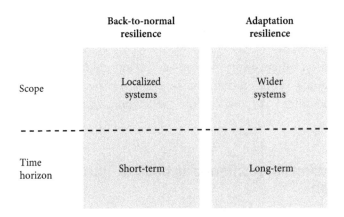

Figure 5.1 Varying approaches to resilience.

repairs than might make them more disaster-proof in the future. Yet much of what happens during a disaster—and the extent of the resilience to it—is determined in the pre- and post-disaster phases. This work in the pre- and post-disaster phases is not dominated by the sense of urgency that accompanies the immediate aftermath of disaster noted in Chapter 4. In the pre-disaster phase, activities that improve prevention (i.e., measures to avoid loss in the first place), mitigation (i.e., measures to limit losses), and prepared-ness (i.e., measures to make sure that response is timely and appropriate to avoid losses getting worse) are crucial. For instance, the availability of mobile flood defenses and the ability to deploy them quickly can dramatically reduce the damage from floods. In the post-disaster phase, the ability to learn from disaster is crucial to further improve prevention, mitigation, preparedness, and response.

When resilience is seen as adaptation, connections are made across all the phases of the disaster cycle: putting in place prevention and mitiga-tion measures pre-disaster; making sure that disaster response is adequate to avoid damages escalating; and, post-disaster, learning from the experience of the current disaster to limit damage at the next occurrence. Indeed, the post-disaster phase of one disaster becomes the pre-disaster phase of the next.

A final set of complexities arises because disasters are multipliers of inequality. Those with access to resources emerge from crises faster and in better condition. Those who do not tend to experience an escalation of the negative consequences of disaster.[6] Unequally distributed resilience is, therefore, a further multiplier of inequality,[7] raising questions about how to allocate resources for resilience across society, not just across phases and timeframes.

5.2.2 Insurance and resilience

Insurance has traditionally fit neatly with a back-to-normal approach to resilience. The funds it releases allow policyholders, post-disaster, to restore their properties to their pre-disaster condition, thus going back to their nor-mal life as quickly as possible. As one insurer mused to us, a back-to-normal approach sets the boundary of insurance:

> We always get asked why insurers do not fund what we call betterment, like improving peoples' homes when they're flooded to make them more resilient to flooding in the future. It's because insurance is there to put you back in the place where you were before. You had the home, it got damaged, you've put it back to

what it was like before. But we're not improving your home. You're not profiting out of your insurance claim, even if that might make you more resilient to flooding and make you a better risk in the future.

(Interview—Insurance Industry)

If placed within a disaster risk management framework, the traditional role of insurance is thus focused on "financial protection" (see Pillar 4 in Figure 5.2). High levels of insurance can provide financial resilience by making funds available for reconstruction, ensuring that economic recovery is not stymied by difficulties in accessing finance. Conversely, insurance that is unequally distributed can worsen inequality.[8] Whether equally or unequally distributed, by providing financial resilience, traditional insurance works in the post-disaster phase, to enable the short-term, narrow-scope response of return-to-normal resilience (see Figure 5.1).

Insurance can, however, also foster pre-disaster mitigation and post-disaster adaptation by helping to build knowledge about and incentivize "physical resilience": non-financial measures that mitigate or prevent damage and thus also economic losses (see Pillars 1, 2, 3, and 5 in Figure 5.2). Typical examples of measures that increase physical resilience include building codes requiring materials and designs that are less prone to damage,

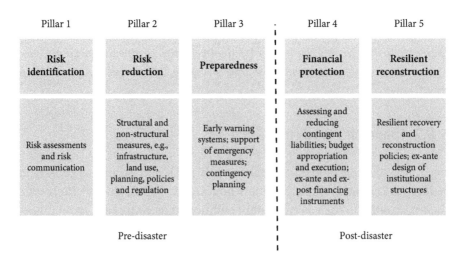

Figure 5.2 The disaster risk management framework
(adapted from Ghesquiere, F., Mahul, O., "Financial Protection of the State Against Natural Disasters: A Primer." Policy research working paper no. 5429. Washington, DC: World Bank; 2010. Available from: http://hdl.handle.net/10986/3912, World Bank, *The Sendai Report: Managing Disaster Risks for a Resilient Future*. Washington, DC: 2012. Available from: https://openknowledge.worldbank.org/handle/10986/23745)

and disaster-aware land-use planning.[9] The insurance industry role in such measures has developed along two trajectories.

The first is to assist in a limited move from back-to-normal toward adaptation, through insurance premium discounts to incentivize mitigation measures either at the construction stage or at the point of reconstruction after disaster. For example, in flood-prone areas buildings that are designed with their heating systems above the predicted level of flood, rather than the more traditional basement location, would qualify for a discount on their flood insurance premium. While the use of these kinds of measures is slowly growing,[10] they are not common.[11] This is partly a problem of knowledge; the insurance industry has knowledge around the costs associated with disaster damage but is less able to calculate precisely deductions that might be applied over the insured life of a property to reflect resilience measures.[12]

These measures also generate tensions because they shift a considerable part of the responsibility to avoid risk onto individuals rather than onto the government. The focus is on the building and what individuals can do to improve the resilience of the building rather than on broader systemic measures such as flood levies or building standards. Yet, individual property owners often have difficulty in finding the right information and clarifying any specific action they might take that would lead to reduced premiums.[13] Even when the information is available, individuals might not have the money to invest in improvements to the resilience of their homes.[14] This shifting of responsibility to individuals is a multiplier of inequality in terms of both insurance and resilience. Those who are more disadvantaged are less likely to have either the ability to insure or to adopt the mitigation measures that might make them more insurable.[15]

The second potential role for insurance in resilience is to take a stronger step toward adaptation by tackling the interdependencies between government and the insurance industry. That is, developing a system where insurance stakeholders and government work together to tackle resilience. For example, using insurance data to inform local government land-use policies or tying in policies of chimney removal in earthquake-prone areas with insurance premium reductions, with government funds to support these modifications for less wealthy households. Integration of insurance with these types of building and environmental measures can help reduce damage.[16] They need to be applied systematically, with a view to long-term adaptation, as the intersecting challenges of the climate crisis and demographic trends, particularly urbanization, place an ever-larger share of the population at risk of disaster.[17] This calls for a strong government role in mandating building standards and other systemic measures, such as land-use planning. There is a potential role for insurance disaster risk modeling to inform these government initiatives. For example, industry expertise in modeling economic losses arising from disaster could be an important input to the pre-disaster activities of risk identification and assessment at policy levels (see Pillar 1 in Figure 5.2).[18]

There are thus opportunities for insurance to support a shift toward systemic adaptation. However, these opportunities contradict insurance's traditional role of enabling a return-to-normal that might well perpetuate and increase vulnerability to disaster.[19] The potential damage of a return-to-normal approach is particularly evident when the climate crisis is considered. For example, the insurance claims payments in the aftermath of Australian bushfires, cyclones, and floods increased vulnerability in disaster-prone areas by enabling rebuilding, whilst the underlying climate exposure was neglected.[20] Moving beyond this traditional role involves a difficult and fundamental shift. The insurance industry needs to engage in complicated discussions with a much wider range of stakeholders, including the most vulnerable parts of the population that typically do not benefit from either pre-disaster mitigation or insurance.[21] In addition, a wider knowledge base must be developed around how resilience can be factored into insurance products and pricing practices.[22] Shifting the insurance industry to being a partner in resilience-as-adaptation is a fundamental change for the industry, its knowledge base, and its relationships with other stakeholders. It requires a fundamental rethinking of the control paradox in terms of how the insurance market provides societal benefits for protection. It requires a fundamental rethinking of the responsibility paradox in terms of how both individuals and the collective can be supported to achieve physical and financial resilience. Unsurprisingly, therefore, the insurance industry reaction, as shown in our initial vignette, is often to push the issue of resilience onto other parties and just keep doing what insurers have always done, especially when commitment from other stakeholders, particularly the government, is unclear.[23]

In summary, the insurance industry is traditionally grounded in the short-term, return-to-normal approach to resilience. In the context of a climate crisis this might end up exacerbating vulnerabilities and increasing inequality. While insurance has some tools to support a long-term, systemic adaptation response, the insurance industry's engagement in resilience has so far been only partial, due to mismatches in knowledge bases and difficulties in either exerting control over, or changing responsibility for, a resilience-as-adaptation response. In the next section, we argue that PGEs can help extend the insurance system's reach into resilience. We show how PGEs' roles can range from limited impact on adaptation, similar to private-sector insurers, to a full partner role in the broader adaptation approach to resilience.

5.3 PGEs' role in resilience

PGEs are established to address problems in insurability, but it is becoming increasingly clear that to deliver on this they also need to grapple with the thorny issue of resilience. As one insurance industry participant reflected:

> The whole idea is to set this [PGE] up to give a window of opportunity to change things and reduce people's risk. If you don't do anything, then that risk-reflective pricing is going to look pretty bad for these high-risks, right? And you'll just have unaffordable premiums again.
>
> **(Interview—Insurance Industry)**

PGEs straddle the boundaries between the government and the insurance industry. They have unique capabilities in building knowledge about potential future protection gaps, and connections to both private- and public-sector partners they can use to search for a new equilibrium to address those future gaps (Chapter 4). PGEs are thus uniquely placed to play an important role in weaving together the multiple threads of resilience. The extent to which they can exploit their unique position depends on how easily their remit enables them to focus on overall resilience and thus use insurance as a tool in the service of physical resilience. Different PGE remits lead to different engagement with the phases of the disaster cycle, different degrees of interconnectedness with other stakeholders operating in the resilience landscape, and, ultimately, different outcomes in facilitating either adaptation or back-to-normal resilience.

We now examine two main patterns by which PGEs engage with resilience; one in which financial resilience dominates and one in which it is integrated with physical resilience.

5.3.1 Privileging financial resilience through insurance markets

Some PGEs have a remit that is targeted overwhelmingly toward finding new ways to package risk so that it can be transferred from some sector of the population to insurance markets (see Appendix A). A dominant focus on financial resilience leads these PGEs to reproduce the limitations of the insurance industry in dealing with physical resilience. Regardless of whether the control paradox is balanced in favor of the industry or the government, and the responsibility paradox is balanced in favor of individual or collective responsibility, such PGEs tend to have limited impact on physical resilience.

An example of a PGE that adopts a government intervention and collective approach and has a remit focused on financial resilience is Consorcio de Compensación de Seguros (Consorcio). Consorcio is designed to replace the disaster insurance market almost entirely and provides compulsory disaster insurance at the same price for the same type of property (e.g., home, offices, commercial buildings) to all property policyholders in Spain. They see themselves primarily as insurers, with limited responsibility for resilience, which is considered the responsibility of other stakeholders: "a criticism we receive is that we are not contributing to risk-mitigation, and we are not lowering risk . . . As a public institution [and thus with a duty to the country], we are happy to be part of that, but it is the role of other institutions to lead in this area" (Interview—PGE). Thus, traditionally, Consorcio's role in physical resilience has been limited. Its major contribution—the power to demand improvements at the reconstruction stage for properties that suffer significant and repeated damage—is used infrequently.

In recent years, as resilience has come to the forefront, Consorcio has steadily increased collaboration with other partners in the resilience ecosystem. Initial efforts included sharing its data on disaster losses with other government stakeholders, such as the Directorate for Civil Protection and Emergencies, who can then use it in their own activities (see Pillar 1 in Figure 5.2). More recently, Consorcio has collaborated with other government agencies to produce guides on how to prevent damage from floods and contributed its risk expertise to pilot prevention projects led by the Ministry for Ecological Transition.[24] Consorcio is thus increasingly active as a partner in physical resilience, supporting progress led by others, but in a limited and sporadic fashion, rather than being fully integrated within the resilience ecosystem in Spain.

This lack of integration with a broad array of stakeholders in the resilience ecosystem also arises for many PGEs in a context of industry control over the market and an emphasis on individual responsibility for protection (see Chapter 3). Such PGEs have a primary duty to provide insurance with the least possible disruption to insurance markets, even when physical resilience is an explicit, but secondary, remit. California Earthquake Authority (CEA) is an example. To avoid interfering in the competitive market, its remit initially focused on providing insurance at prices that reflect the true nature of the risk (see Chapter 3). However, soon after, a second component related to incentivizing individuals to adopt physical resilience measures was added to its remit. Today CEA pursues resilience by partially financing retrofitting of houses (whether insured or not) to make them more resilient to earthquake; "we're doing thousands of retrofits now" (Interview—PGE). Any such retrofitted houses that took up insurance were offered premium discounts.

CEA's resilience remit involves a limited expansion over the traditional understanding of insurance as back-to-normal, with a strict focus on the individual property owner's building and with little engagement with the overall physical resilience system of the government. Thus, its move into the resilience landscape is along the lines of the insurance industry, with a focus on limited adaptation that is centered on the individual building. CEA struggles to join forces with other stakeholders and activate important levers of physical resilience at the wider system level, such as what housing is built and where. This inability to engage more widely hampers their ability to influence long-term, systemic adaptation.

The dominant remit for both Consorcio and CEA is financial resilience. While they differ in the balance of control between industry or government (see Chapters 3 and 4), this is not key to their effect on physical resilience, so much as the fact that they are in place primarily to provide insurance. As Consorcio does not adopt risk-reflective pricing, its approach blunts any incentives for individuals to increase physical resilience to lower their premiums. Dealing with resilience is largely left to government. For CEA, the risk-reflective pricing of its insurance should discourage construction in high-risk areas by contributing to lower house prices, due to the high-risk and high insurance costs. Yet, as we have shown above, in practice insurance is not particularly direct or effective in promoting physical resilience.[25] While premium prices reflect the risk, people cannot simply relocate or rebuild. For social and financial reasons, they usually cannot afford to.[26] Thus, as in California with earthquake insurance, they simply drop out of the insurance market. In both cases, the PGEs are not engaged in substantive changes toward resilience-as-adaptation, which is left mostly in the hands of government stakeholders, such as the offices that oversee land use.

These examples show that a primary remit to provide insurance constrains a PGE's possibility to impact resilience. This, rather than how they balance industry versus government control or individual versus collective responsibility (Chapter 3), limits the work a PGE can do to address the long-term threat of disequilibrium. Being primarily a vehicle for insurance does not help PGEs to reshape wider relationships that would promote a new equilibrium, in which more properties are protected physically from disaster. Such PGEs may play a role in post-disaster recovery and can even move beyond return-to-normal—but they are not dominant players in long-term adaptation.

5.3.2 Can a PGE move from financial to physical resilience?

Some PGEs, which were set up with a remit tightly focused on financial resilience, can actively seek to work around the constraints it poses to their engagement in physical resilience. We explore this situation through the example of Flood Re.

Flood Re's remit is clearly and narrowly defined: to provide insurance cover for 25 years for a limited number of properties that are classified as most at risk of flood. At the end of this period, Flood Re is mandated to return these properties to a market where they have access to affordable, risk-reflective insurance. This remit required Flood Re to set up a risk register, collecting information for its own risk management, so it could assess risk-reflective pricing for the properties it was to cover. Upon its establishment, Flood Re's first step was thus to improve its understanding of the risk via better modeling (see Pillar 1 in Figure 5.2). As one participant explained:

> One of the biggest component parts of our work was further investigation of the flood models and what we like, what we do not like with them, what are they covering, what are they not covering, etc. And that was really useful because we've moved ourselves on with respect to our understanding of the risk. . . . So, we have made inroads into the whole objective of Flood Re, which is to make the understanding of risk better.
>
> **(Interview—PGE)**

As Flood Re increased its understanding of these risks, it quickly recognized a pending future disequilibrium; it would be impossible to deliver the exit strategy without a major change in physical resilience that lowered the risk of these properties and thus also their premiums. However, as Flood Re's initial remit did not include resilience, it could not discount for resilience features, incentivize resilient reconstruction after disaster, nor directly influence any decision regarding land-use planning or building permission. As a participant observed reflecting on their limited ability to influence wider, long-term adaptive measures:

> All the evidence says that pre-disaster [physical] resilience at a community level is more effective than post-disaster [physical] resilience at house level. But, given

our remit, it's very difficult for us to jump into a community and go "right, OK, we're going to pay for this wall because we think that'll give the best bang for the buck."

(Interview—PGE)

Flood Re managers thus began to shift their focus to physical resilience and to engage with those stakeholders responsible for it. They expanded their sphere of activity to the pre- and post-disaster phases in a two-pronged approach. First, they connected directly with policyholders to raise awareness of resilience measures and support them in their individual efforts to become more flood resilient. They built a "Floodmobile"; a mobile home that showcased ways to make properties more flood resilient and toured through the UK's most flood-prone areas. While this addressed some elements of the prevention part of the disaster cycle, it placed the onus on the individual to undertake property mitigation. On its own, it would not be enough for long-term adaptation. Second, therefore, they lobbied alongside other stakeholders, through activities such as speaking on resilience at COP 26.[27] They also pushed for government action, for example, through submissions to parliamentary calls for evidence following flooding disasters:[28]

> It's really just about saying: what views do we have on the effectiveness of resilience of properties and where do we want to start influencing others like the Environment Agency and government and others. . . . The biggest challenge we have is that we can't use our money to invest in flood defenses. That's got to be done by the Environment Agency.

(Interview—PGE)

By working to raise awareness amongst stakeholders of the threat of a persistent disequilibrium in the insurance market, Flood Re began reshaping the system to make resilience more central. They began to use insurance in the service of resilience, and to support individuals to take responsibility for their resilience, by gaining the authority to finance a "Build Back Better" program from April 2022. This program supports localized adaptation, as it enables flood insurance claims to be used to make individual houses more resilient to disaster. Nonetheless, Flood Re still lacks connections and authority in other crucial processes such as the definition of land use, the development of flood defenses, and the building permit process. In addition, some properties might not be economically salvageable despite mitigation efforts, given the trends projected for the climate crisis.[29]

It is thus crucial that Flood Re continues its work to construct a new equilibrium in which stakeholders who have more control over the resilience landscape, such as planning permission and flood defenses, support a more collective responsibility for resilience. Through such actions, Flood Re's might expand its own remit to use insurance as a tool in the pursuit of physical as well as financial resilience. Given the pressures to build new houses in the UK,[30] and the barriers that the largely industry-oriented approach puts in the way of PGE evolution, this will require significant political skills in using the knowledge they generate (see Chapter 4) to influence long-term system adaptation.

5.3.3 Integrating financial and physical resilience

Let us introduce the rare contrasting case to the above. Some PGEs have a more expansive remit that focuses on insurance as a tool in achieving overall resilience. This enables them to play a more proactive role. The Swiss system of disaster insurance, based on cantonal PGEs, is an example that shows how the responsibility and control paradoxes (Chapter 3) can be reconfigured to be more conducive to a higher overall resilience.

Switzerland adopts a dual system with part of the country relying on highly regulated private provision, and part of the country (accounting for about 80 percent of the market by both value and number of buildings)[31] relying on cantonal-level public-sector insurers who operate local monopolies. These 19 cantonal PGEs are not-for-profit public-sector organizations, without a government guarantee, and operationally independent from the state. Each of these PGEs provides insurance for multiple different types of disaster, which is compulsory and is offered at the same price (a percentage of insured value) to any building within the canton. Disaster insurance coverage is thus virtually complete.

These cantonal insurers historically started by providing fire insurance and firefighting services, with disaster insurance gradually added from the 1920s.[32] The historical link with fire insurance and firefighting has made resilience considerations, particularly a focus on timely and appropriate response, also integral to their approach to disaster insurance.

The links between financial and physical resilience were further strengthened following a wave of natural disasters in the 1990s which led to the development of an integrated national risk-management system. Today, the provision of insurance is, therefore, seen as just one component of the role of the system of PGEs.

The real unique aspect of our system is that we cover three parts. We have prevention, we have intervention, and insurance. As we are public institutions, we can put obligations on policyholders to do protection measures. We do a lot of prevention work. With good prevention you have less damage. . . . We supervise the fire brigades and so can make sure that they have the right equipment, the right education to do the work well and to limit possible damage. And the third part, the damage that occurs, we cover it with insurance. And this triangle is key to our system.

(Interview—PGE)

A significant part of the cantonal insurers' budget, financed by their premiums, goes into prevention of damage, including financing improvements to properties that have been subjected to heavy or recurrent losses, and the training and equipment of fire brigades. As they explain: "fire brigades in Switzerland are our first line of defense. They are not only fighting fires. In case of floods, they put up mobile flood defenses. Those are heavily subsidized by the public insurance companies" (Interview—PGE).

Resilience via insurance mechanisms has been implicated in planning. For example, "if you want permission [to build], you need insurance. Then we [at the PGE] look to see if this building has some dangers, and we insist that they adopt prevention measures, to build something different, a little bit larger, higher" (Interview—PGE). This is a particularly effective resilience step for floods, for example, where relatively simple and inexpensive provisions at the design stage can limit losses significantly in the case of moderate floods. The cantonal PGEs also tend to intervene post-disaster, by supporting build-back-better approaches with both advice and partial financing. For example, on individual family dwellings, much mitigation and prevention takes place after disaster.

We have quite a big number of [external] architects who go out after an event to do an estimation of the damage. This is a very effective point of intervention because people realize what we pay is a small part of the personal value which got lost after a flood. Those things are lost forever. So, this arrangement is effective for implementing measures that prevent damage next time.

(Interview—PGE)

These building-centered resilience activities are not unique to the Swiss system. For instance, we have already seen that Flood Re has evolved to include similar "build-back-better" activities and that the CEA also engages in pre-disaster mitigation. The Swiss system's distinctive feature is that these building-centered activities are integrated with disaster response and disaster mitigation across all the pillars of resilience depicted in Figure 5.2, through a myriad of formal and informal ties between PGEs and other stakeholders in the resilience landscape. Government controls are, thus, not simply over the insurance market but over the whole resilience landscape, fostering the relationships between insurance providers and those with responsibility for building codes and planning permission in a comprehensive framework.

This approach acts as a multiplier of the PGEs' impact on longer term systemic adaptation and involves Swiss PGEs interacting with a wide array of resilience stakeholders as an integrated part of the system in the following types of activities:

- Development of building standards by the appropriate authorities and the certification of building materials;
- Collaboration in the local authorities' production of risk maps that are then used to restrict construction in certain areas and require special measures in other risk-prone areas. While owners of properties in high-risk zones benefit from the same insurance prices as everybody else, no new construction is allowed, and old construction cannot be rebuilt;
- Consultations regarding land-use planning;
- Contributing to larger-scale resilience measures, funded by cantonal or national government, through risk assessments based on their knowledge of insurance claims and losses.

Thus, for Swiss PGEs financial and physical resilience support each other. The financial resilience aspect of the PGEs' work remains an integral part of a balanced view of risk, as risk cannot be entirely eliminated:

> Let's say it makes sense from an insurance point to build up walls to address exposure to flooding for a property. You cannot force the homeowner or people living there to live behind flood protection measures that take away all the view and make access to their building very difficult or whatever for hundreds of years. We cannot keep everything safe. So that's the classic insurance part, you have damage to an insured value.
>
> (Interview—PGE)

This integration of physical and financial resilience supports long-term systemic adaptation, consistently enforcing measures to limit damage and integrating measures at the building level with community-level measures. This adaptive approach to resilience makes sharing risk equally across all stakeholders via mandatory disaster insurance feasible. It keeps prices low, provides benefits for everyone, and does not expose the community to continuously financing repeated losses that can be avoided by intervention in physical resilience.

Of course, the Swiss cantonal system is not without limitations. While most natural disasters are insured, there is a significant protection gap in relation to earthquake (see Chapter 4). And PGEs themselves remark how factors such as changes in the design of contemporary buildings, such as the extensive use of glass, and the need to accommodate a growing population are leading to increases in overall risk. Nonetheless, the Swiss system illustrates how responsibility for resilience can be balanced across individuals and the collective through a government that controls the financial role of the insurance industry and its relationships to other private- and public-sector bodies involved in increasing physical resilience. This is a fundamental expansion of the system of control and responsibility that actively integrates financial and physical resilience to disaster.

5.3.4 Can a PGE be designed to integrate financial and physical resilience?

Successful resilience systems are difficult to imitate. They are complex, and their success derives not only from the performance of each of their many individual components (PGEs, land-use planning, infrastructure planning, building permits, construction standards, etc.), but also from their interconnectedness. These interconnections often emerge over a long period of time, sometimes as a happy accident of history. Yet, some newly established PGEs indicate how systems based on similar principles can be built. For example, African Risk Capacity (ARC) started its journey in 2012 grounded in resilience: seeing insurance as effective only when part of a larger resilience landscape. This contrasts with most PGEs, which start from insurance and then attempt to influence the broader resilience framework to sustain their ability to insure.

ARC is a multi-country PGE that focuses on disaster response (see Chapter 4, Case 4.1). Their remit focuses on resilience at the disaster response phase. They aim to ensure the ability of permanently cash-strapped governments to respond rapidly and effectively to disaster, preventing damage from getting worse in the aftermath of disaster. ARC started its operations to provide insurance products to mitigate against the effects of drought in African nations. Providing funds that help drought-stricken populations to weather a drought and to remain on their lands can dramatically reduce the human and economic cost of a drought.[33] However, this is only possible if the funds are dispatched quickly and if they can be transformed into material supplies that are delivered quickly to the affected populations:

> The payout is supposed to be used to address immediate needs. . . . it's an early-action payout . . . it's not, for example, to support people to prepare for farming, you know, it's more for addressing needs of people that have been affected by drought and that are likely to be food-insecure.
>
> **(Interview—Development Agency)**

ARC cannot mitigate the actual incidence of drought. Its aim is to mitigate some of the effects, such as insufficient food, prior to the situation becoming disastrous. Resilience to the effects of drought is built into how the financial product is provided by ARC. Most insurance products trigger after a disaster has occurred, thereby linking into the post-disaster phase of the disaster cycle. By contrast, as drought is a slow-onset disaster, the ARC product triggers before the disaster is in full force. ARC's process is thus about identifying the critical moment in drought onset when a rapid injection of cash can help mitigate its effects. It is thus a disaster risk mitigation approach. It also works pre-disaster to make sure that governments have the processes and structures to use that payment effectively in the response phase (see Figure 5.2, Pillars 1 and 3), thus increasing the resilience of the whole disaster response system. That is the aim of the ARC remit: "most important is how you use this payout to address the immediate need of the population, to address their food security and prevent them having to sell off their assets, the small assets that they have" (Interview—PGE).

The preparation necessary to avert the worst effects of oncoming disaster is key to the purpose of the ARC insurance products. Indeed, ARC has two parts. One is dedicated to the development of insurance products that can be financed in the international reinsurance markets, so supporting financial resilience. The other part supports African country governments in understanding what type of disaster impacts they face, and in developing the operational and contingency plans necessary to deliver aid: "the work that we do helps to guide the government to say 'according to our modelling, these are the areas where the impact is going to be significant; it is in these areas that we are going to start'" (Interview—PGE). Governments can only participate in the insurance scheme once they have developed a viable operational plan for responding to a disaster. When disasters are imminent, they provide a detailed operational plan to ARC for getting food to people before the funds are disbursed. This ensures that mitigation of the disaster effects is integrated with the financial payment.

ARC's bringing even more value because of the contingency planning and the discipline around the use of the funds. There's lots of other value being created just getting Ministries of Finance along with disaster management people in the same room making some decisions in advance . . . before any actual risk transfer happens.

(Interview—PGE)

ARC remains relatively limited in its approach to long-term system-wide adaptive resilience. For example, it cannot help in designing farming systems that are less vulnerable to drought. Nonetheless, it demonstrates how a PGE can be designed to integrate insurance into a resilience framework. By anchoring on response and by putting resilience first, these PGEs are showing an alternative path through which insurance can be a tool in building resilience and adaptation—not the other way round. We hope future PGEs are created with this in mind.

5.4 Conclusion: Integrating financial and physical resilience makes PGEs sustainable

Integrating physical and financial resilience is a critical but difficult role for PGEs as they seek to generate a new long-term sustainable equilibrium in which disaster risk is sufficiently mitigated that it can remain insurable. Most PGEs focus primarily on restoring or developing insurance as a form of protection (see Chapter 2). They therefore struggle to integrate insurance with the physical resilience measures that mitigate the effects of disaster because such efforts are outside their remit. Yet PGEs are faced with the growing threat of disequilibrium (in the form of increasingly complex insurance protection gaps) associated with the climate crisis and changing demographic trends. A key challenge for many PGEs, therefore, is to work through the tensions that arise when their remits are designed to address only one part of the resilience framework.

Working through this challenge holds opportunity, as PGEs are in a unique position to recognize gaps in future provision of protection (Chapter 4). They can use this knowledge to inform resilience measures that help reduce those gaps and ensure the future relevance of PGEs in addressing protection gaps. In doing so, they can circumvent a looming challenge for many PGEs and societies. Insurance uses rising price as a market signal to indicate risk that is increasingly unsustainable and thus needs to be mitigated. PGEs can suppress this market signal through smoothing out the price of insurance. It is true that those "pure" market signals have so far had limited effectiveness in motivating physical resilience.[34] However, suppressing them via PGEs without attention to physical resilience will only contribute to making risks increasingly uninsurable, and thus undermining the mission of PGEs. We therefore advocate for PGEs to reduce the protection gap by integrating their insurance-based financial resilience role with physical resilience. While few PGEs have the long-term systemic capability of the Swiss PGE system discussed here, their activities in knowledge-generation and awareness-raising contribute to the overall potential for greater resilience throughout society— but only if PGEs are more thoroughly embedded within the wide resilience landscape. Thus, even where they are not designed to deliver resilience, or struggle to do so, PGEs' efforts build capability that can be drawn upon at a future point.

5.5 Learning points

1. Interactions between financial and physical resilience. The pursuit of financial resilience can undermine the pursuit of physical resilience. Yet, physical resilience is central to the sustainability of insurance in the face of more serious and frequent disasters. Thus, a key issue that PGEs need to address is how to integrate the two into the core purpose of their remit.
2. The longer term role of a PGE's remit. Insurance implies a return-to-normal view of resilience. This approach is increasingly insufficient to address the challenges of a climate crisis. When the remit of a PGE is dominated by providing insurance, its role in physical resilience will be limited, with few of the interconnections with the stakeholders in the resilience landscape that are needed to foster adaptation. This inability to seriously address resilience will occur whenever insurance is the primary goal, independently of whether the PGE also has an emphasis on collective or individual responsibility for protection and is oriented toward industry or government control over the insurance market.
3. Starting from overall resilience. The PGEs that have more impact on physical resilience start from a view of insurance as part of a resilience system, rather than bolting on resilience after the fact. Insurance via PGEs thus needs to be designed as a tool in the service of overall resilience within our societies.

Notes

1. Pörtner. H.-O., Roberts, D. C., Tignor, M., Poloczanska, E. S., Mintenbeck, K., Alegría, A., Craig, M., Langsdorf, S., Löschke, S., Möller, V., Okem, A., Rama, B., eds, *Climate Change 2022: Impacts, Adaptation and Vulnerability.* IPCC. Contribution of working group II to the sixth assessment report of the intergovernmental panel on climate change. Cambridge: Cambridge University Press, 2022. Available from: https://www.ipcc.ch/report/ar6/wg2/downloads/report/IPCC_AR6_WGII_FullReport.pdf

2. Elliott, R., *Underwater: Loss, Flood Insurance, and the Moral Economy of Climate Change in the United States.* New York: Columbia University Press, 2021.

3. Martin-Breen, P., Anderies, J. M., *Resilience: A Literature Review.* Bellagio Initiative. Brighton: IDS, 2011. Available from: https://opendocs.ids.ac.uk/opendocs/handle/20.500.12413/3692

4. Hutter, B. M., ed., *Risk, Resilience, Inequality and Environmental Law.* Cheltenham: Edward Elgar Publishing, 2017, 207–27.

5. Bosher, L., Chmutina, K., van Niekerk, D., "Stop Going around in Circles: Towards a Reconceptualisation of Disaster Risk Management Phases." *Disaster Prevention and Management,* 30(4/5) (2021): 525–37. https://doi.org/10.1108/DPM-03-2021-0071.

    Alexander, D. E., *Principles of Emergency Planning and Management.* Dunedin: Terra Publishing, 2002.

6. Howell, J., Elliott, J. R., "Damages Done: The Longitudinal Impacts of Natural Hazards on Wealth Inequality in the United States." *Social Problems,* 66(3) (2019): 448–67. https://doi.org/10.1093/socpro/spy016

7. Gotham, K. F., Greenberg, M., *Crisis Cities: Disaster and Redevelopment in New York and New Orleans.* Oxford: Oxford University Press, 2014.

    Knighton, J., Hondula, K., Sharkus, C., Guzman, C., Elliott, R., "Flood Risk Behaviors of United States Riverine Metropolitan Areas are Driven by Local Hydrology and Shaped by Race." *Proceedings of the National Academy of Sciences,* 118(13) (2021): e2016839118. https://doi.org/10.1073/pnas.2016839118

8. Booth, K., Tranter, B., "When Disaster Strikes: Under-Insurance in Australian Households." *Urban Studies,* 55(14) (2018): 3135–50. https://doi.org/10.1177/00420980 17736257

9. For instance, Bowker, P., Escarameia, M., Tagg, A., *Improving the Flood Performance of New Buildings: Flood Resilient Construction.* London: Department of Communities and Local Government and DEFRA/Environment Agency Flood Risk Management Research and Development program, 2007. Available from: https://assets.publishing.service.gov.uk/media/602d673ee90e0709e8d085d8/Improving_the_Flood_Resilience_of_Buildings_Through_Improved_Materials__Methods_and_Details_Technical_Report.pdf

10. de Vet, E., Eriksen, C., Booth, K., French, S., "An Unmitigated Disaster: Shifting from Response and Recovery to Mitigation for an Insurable Future." *International Journal of Disaster Risk Science,* 10(2) (2019): 179–92. https://doi.org/10.1007/s13753-019-0214-0.

    Thieken, A. H., Kienzler, S., Kreibich, H., Kuhlicke, C., Kunz, M., Mühr, B., Müller, M., Otto, A., Petrow, T., Pisi, S., Schröter, K., "Review of the Flood Risk Management System in Germany after the Major Flood in 2013." *Ecology and Society*, 21(2) (2016): 51. https://www.jstor.org/stable/26270411

11. Hudson, P., De Ruig, L. T., de Ruiter, M. C., Kuik, O. J., Botzen, W. W., Le Den, X., Persson, M., Benoist, A., Nielsen, C. N., "An Assessment of Best Practices of Extreme Weather Insurance and Directions for a More Resilient Society." *Environmental Hazards*, 19(3) (2020): 301–21. https://doi.org/10.1080/17477891.2019.1608148.

    Javeline, D., Kijewski-Correa, T., "Coastal Homeowners in a Changing Climate." *Climatic Change*, 152(2) (2019): 259–74. https://doi.org/10.1007/s10584-018-2257-4.

    Surminski, S., Thieken, A. H., "Promoting Flood Risk Reduction: The Role of Insurance in Germany and England." *Earth's Future*, 5(10) (2017): 979–1001. https://doi.org/10.1002/2017EF000587

12. Hudson, P., Botzen, W. J. W., Feyen, L., Aerts, J. C. J. H., "Incentivizing Flood Risk Adaptation through Risk-Based Insurance Premiums: Trade-offs between Affordability and Risk Reduction." *Ecological Economics*, 125 (2016): 1–13. https://doi.org/10.1016/j.ecolecon.2016.01.015.

    Keskitalo, E. C. H., Juhola, S., Baron, N., Fyhn, H., Klein, J., "Implementing Local Climate Change Adaptation and Mitigation Actions: The Role of Various Policy Instruments in a Multi-Level Governance Context." *Climate*, 4(1) (2016): 7. https://doi.org/10.3390/cli4010007

13. Kousky, C., *Understanding Disaster Insurance: New Tools for a More Resilient Future*. Washington, DC: Island Press, 2022.

14. De Vet et al., "Unmitigated Disaster." Elliott,. *Underwater*.

15. Gotham, K. F., Greenberg, M., *Crisis Cities: Disaster and Redevelopment in New York and New Orleans*. Oxford: Oxford University Press, 2014.

    Knighton et al., "Flood Risk Behaviors."

16. Poussin, J. K., Bubeck, P., Aerts, J. C. J. H., Ward, P. J., "Potential of Semi-Structural and Non-Structural Adaptation Strategies to Reduce Future Flood Risk: Case Study for the Meuse." *Natural Hazards and Earth System Sciences*, 12(11) (2012): 3455–71. https://doi.org/10.5194/nhess-12-3455-2012

17. Pörtner et al., *Climate Change 2022*.

    Perrow, C., *The Next Catastrophe: Reducing our Vulnerabilities to Natural, Industrial, and Terrorist Disasters*. Princeton: Princeton University Press, 2011.

    Schanz, K.-U., *Future Urban Risk Landscapes: An Insurance Perspective*. Geneva: Geneva Association, 2021. Available from: https://www.genevaassociation.org/research-topics/socio-economic-resilience/future-urban-risk-landscapes-insurance-perspective

18. Collier, S. J., Cox, S., "Governing Urban Resilience: Insurance and the Problematization of Climate Change." *Economy and Society*, 50(2) (2021): 275–96. https://doi.org/10.1080/03085147.2021.1904621

19. Christophers, B., "The Allusive Market: Insurance of Flood Risk in Neoliberal Britain." *Economy and Society*, 48(1): 1–29. https://doi.org/10.1080/03085147.2018.1547494.

    O'Hare, P., White, I., Connelly, A., "Insurance as Maladaptation: Resilience and the 'Business as Usual' Paradox." *Environment and Planning C: Government and Policy*, 34(6) (2016): 1175–93. https://doi.org/10.1177/0263774X15602022

20. De Vet et al., "Unmitigated Disaster."

21. De Vet et al., "Unmitigated Disaster."

22. Kousky, *Understanding Disaster Insurance.*

23. Christophers, "Allusive Market."

24. Ferreiro, P., Rambla, A., Aparicio, M., Francisco Arrazola, J., *Pilot Cases for Adapting to Flood Risk.* Madrid: Conseguros, 2020, no. 12. Available from: https://www.consorsegurosdigital.com/en/numero-12/front-page/pilot-cases-for-adapting-to-flood-risk

25. Kousky, *Understanding Disaster Insurance.*

26. Singh, R., "Seismic Risk and House Prices: Evidence from Earthquake Fault Zoning." *Regional Science and Urban Economics*, 75 (2019): 187–209. https://doi.org/10.1016/j.regsciurbeco.2019.02.001

27. Flood Re, *Flood Re COP26 hub.* Date accessed: September 2022. Available from: https://www.floodre.co.uk/cop26-hub

28. Flood Re, *Written Evidence Submitted by Flood Re (FLO0061).* London: Flood Re, 2019. Available from: https://committees.parliament.uk/writtenevidence/5681/pdf

29. Sayers, P., Moss, C., Carr, S., Payo Garcia, A., "Responding to Climate Change around England's Coast: The Scale of the Transformational Challenge." *Ocean and Coastal Management*, 2022: 225. https://doi.org/10.1016/j.ocecoaman.2022.106187

30. Rözer, V., Surminski, S., "Current and Future Flood Risk of New Build Homes across Different Socio-Economic Neighborhoods in England and Wales." *Environmental Research Letters*, 16(5) (2021): 054021. https://doi.org/10.1088/1748-9326/abec04

31. VKG, SVV, "Joint Project on Earthquake Insurance." Internal communication; May 10, 2022.

Jarzabkowski, P., Cacciatori, E., Chalkias, K., Gallagher Rodgers, R., *Disaster Insurance in Switzerland: The Cantonal Public Sector Insurance System.* London: Bayes Business School, City, University of London & The University of Queensland, 2022.

32. Wanner, C., *Vorbeugen—Schützen—Entschädigen: Die entstehung der elementarschadenversicherung in der Schweiz.* Bern: Historisches Institut—Universität Bern; 2002.

33. Clarke, D. J., Dercon, S., *Dull Disasters? How Planning ahead will Make a Difference.* Oxford: Oxford University Press, 2016.

Dempsey, B., Hillier, D., *A Dangerous Delay: The Cost of Late Response to Early Warnings in the 2011 Drought in the Horn of Africa.* Inter-Agency Briefing Paper. London: Save the Children and Oxfam, 2012. Available from: https://policy-practice.oxfam.org/resources/a-dangerous-delay-the-cost-of-late-response-to-early-warnings-in-the-2011-droug-203389/

34. Kousky, *Understanding Disaster Insurance.*

6

Reimagining disaster insurance

Toward a new equilibrium

Introductory Case

Is disaster insurance broken? The 2022 Australian floods. As we were writing this book in early 2022, Australia was experiencing the worst flood in its recorded history. This catastrophe affected 1,100 km of the East Coast, causing 22 deaths, mass evacuations, and devastation of homes and infrastructure including in two of Australia's most populated cities. On a balcony well back from the water's edge, one of us sat in transfixed horror watching as the Brisbane River rose, sweeping property and foliage away in its path. As the rain finally eased, it became apparent that many people in the affected areas were uninsured. Insurance had been largely unaffordable for many since premiums jumped in 2011, following extreme floods that killed 33 people and caused insured losses of AUD $2.38 bn (~US $2.43 bn).[1] This time, however, as the waters rose above rooftops and people were evacuated, a proposal for a Northern Australian flood and cyclone Protection Gap Entity (PGE) was going through legislation in Australia. Sadly, even if the PGE had already been in place, it would have had no effect for the flooded population in 2022. The proposed PGE had been so tightly defined that neither the nature of the flood (not caused by a cyclone) nor its location (outside Northern Australia) was within its remit.

The disaster response and recovery were accompanied by the usual blame games. An Insurance Council of Australia spokesperson claimed that "there is no area of Australia that is uninsurable, although there are some locations where there are clearly affordability and availability concerns." Laying the responsibility for addressing the problem elsewhere, the spokesperson claimed: "that is why the Insurance Council has called on all Australian governments to do more to protect homes, businesses and communities from the impacts of extreme weather."[2] At the same time, analysts and insurance companies began to signal that insurance premiums, already unaffordable for many, would have to rise after this

Disaster Insurance Reimagined. Paula Jarzabkowski et al., Oxford University Press. © Paula Jarzabkowski, Konstantinos Chalkias, Eugenia Cacciatori, and Rebecca Bednarek (2023). DOI: 10.1093/oso/9780192865168.003.0006

disaster.[3] While some politicians called for an expansion of the proposed PGE to help address uninsurability, the insurance industry continued to claim that "a flood reinsurance pool is not required at this time."[4]

Further contradictions abounded. The coordinator-general of the National Recovery and Resilience Agency proposed that homes should not be rebuilt in areas that would never be resilient to extreme flooding. Yet, less than a week after the cessation of flooding, with uninhabitable homes still full of stinking mud, the NSW Planning Minister revoked a requirement to consider flood and fire risks before building new homes. His spokesperson cited "priorities to deliver a pipeline of new housing supply and act on housing affordability."[5] Climate scientists pointed to the increasing likelihood of extreme weather disasters, while engineers emphasized the growing vulnerability of properties to such disasters. As the massive task of clean up and recovery began, yet again, the weaknesses in the former strategy of spending money rushing back-to-normal after a disaster, rather than investing in adaptation (see Chapter 5), were apparent.[6]

In September 2022, the Bureau of Meteorology announced a third La Niña extreme wet season, striking fear into the hearts of those still in temporary accommodation from the earlier flooding. The insurance industry was also severely affected. Even with widespread underinsurance, the projected AUD \$5.45 bn[7] (~US \$3.65 bn) in losses from the 2022 flooding more than doubled those in 2011.[8] With more extreme rainfall on the way, how could insurance continue to be a robust solution to finance disaster recovery and reconstruction? Would this finally be the catalyst for fundamental change in an insurance and resilience system that was vastly inadequate for protecting either the population or the economy?

6.1 Introduction

This and similar stories playing out around the world prompt us to ask: how relevant does the global insurance industry want to be in a world of increasing catastrophic disasters? The Australian floods are not the only record-breaking disasters that have occurred while we were writing this book. Among other extreme-weather disasters, wildfires devastated close to 7 million acres of California in 2020 and 2021,[9] much of Europe experienced unprecedented heatwaves in 2022,[10] and the worst drought in decades brought extreme hunger to 18 million people throughout the Horn of Africa.[11] Yet, the insurance industry often appears to have few tools to address such extreme disasters, beyond increasing prices and withdrawing availability. If the global insurance industry continues to retreat from extreme disaster through high pricing and withdrawal while the risk of that disaster continues to grow, its significance will dwindle. As the population at risk of disaster grows, insurance will fall short of its role of providing the safety net that is so fundamental to the working and prosperity of modern societies (Chapter 1).

Insurance matters and we need it to work.[12] The global property insurance market underpins individual and business lending, supports the global movement of goods, and pays for recovery after a disaster.[13] A robust insurance industry benefits individuals and governments. These benefits are economic. Each percentage point increase in property insurance in a country reduces disaster-recovery times by almost 12 months.[14] The benefits are also social. Extensive insurance enables disaster-affected people to return to their normal lives within approximately 12 months.[15] For example, if we consider the case of the Earthquake Commission (EQC) in New Zealand (which opened Chapter 1), the 2010/2011 Christchurch earthquakes caused enormous damage, loss of life, livelihood, and homes. The claims distribution was traumatic, and people suffered. And yet, some 75 percent of those losses were paid through a combination of public- and private-sector insurance, enabling New Zealanders to rebuild homes and businesses, and get back to work, community, and everyday life … until the next disaster.

The role of insurance as a foundation that enables the continuation of taken-for-granted individual economic activities, such as mortgages and home ownership, and global activities, such as trade credit and supply chains, is largely hidden. If disaster insurance dwindles in advanced economies, it will alter the fabric of society. Personal wealth and housing security (often of the most vulnerable) will reduce, and inequality will increase as access to affordable insurance is a key element of social and financial inclusion.[16] If insurance fails to take hold in poorer countries, where there is already less insurance than in rich countries, their road to economic development will be further stunted.[17] In this chapter, we sketch out the potential obsolescence of disaster insurance. We then imagine a way to avoid sleepwalking into a future in which viable disaster insurance can no longer be taken-for-granted.

6.2 The obsolescence of private-sector disaster insurance

This book has shown how disequilibrium among three entangled paradoxes—knowledge, control, and responsibility—makes disasters uninsurable within the private sector. Catastrophic disasters are increasing in severity, frequency, and concurrence due to a complex and compounding set of factors.[18] These include climate change and its interaction with other key factors in a globally interdependent world,[19] such as increasing urbanization, with a global population that has grown by more than 397 million people between 2015 and 2020.[20]

Even in countries with a well-established insurance sector, private-sector insurance is already struggling to continue to insure disasters like flooding,[21] as shown by the development and evolution of PGEs in this book (see Chapters 2 and 4). In the face of this compounding risk of disasters, private-sector insurance faces potential obsolescence as a critical partner in addressing these big risks facing society.

6.2.1 Why is private-sector disaster insurance potentially obsolescent?

Disaster risk is geographically concentrated and affects multiple types of insurance at the same time (for instance, property but also health insurance). Disasters are thus more difficult to insure than other risks, such as car theft, because they create infrequent but large and concentrated losses that can put insurers at risk of default. Disaster insurance thus requires mechanisms for spreading this highly concentrated risk. The birth of global reinsurance markets (in which insurance companies could insure themselves against excessive losses) was a key factor in the growth of disaster insurance.[22] The interconnectedness of economic activities today means, however, that "local" disasters increasingly have the potential to destabilize global supply chains. Climate change and the growth in urbanization mean that increasingly severe cyclones, bushfires, and floods cause losses to high-value assets and large populations in multiple countries with greater frequency.[23] The global insurance industry can only absorb so much of these severe losses within any year, even by transferring these risks from individual people into a collective comprising the entire global insured population and the pot of market capital that provides (see Appendix A).

Insurers and analysts have been highlighting the increasing threat of climate change and other systemic risks to the insurance business model.[24] These studies point to the effects of rising insurance claims globally, the increasing unaffordability and withdrawal of insurance, and the need to limit climate change whilst making greater investment in resilient property and planning. As one of our interviewees noted: "you need to invest a billion pounds a year more on flood risk, just to keep pace with climate change" (Interview—Insurance Industry). Yet, as another participant lamented, it is hard to know whether such investment in property resilience will actually improve insurance affordability or availability: "you imagine the problem of modeling it, what's climate-change-related, how do you price it, what market is interested in it, what sort of premiums; [it's] too high a level of uncertainty" (Interview—Government). Insurers are clear that more action is needed to increase the resilience of assets to climate change and other disasters. Yet they have little control over these actions or how to incorporate them into a viable risk transfer process (see Chapter 5).

6.2.2 COVID-19 indicated the limitations of the insurance system

The COVID-19 pandemic was a disaster that crossed national borders, affecting many types of business and most aspects of civil society. It thus displayed the complex interdependencies and cascading effects characteristic of systemic risk.[25] As the Chartered Insurance Institute noted; "systemic risks—risks, such as COVID-19, that are so large in scale they can cause the breakdown of an entire system—not only pose a major threat to society but also render traditional risk-transfer mechanisms unsuitable, calling into question the role of the insurance sector in addressing them."[26] Many of the economic losses of the COVID-19 pandemic were not insured. Where they were, for example in event cancellation or in business interruption, the insurance industry was reluctant to pay for a disaster it would never knowingly have insured. This generated litigation around the world.[27] Insurers pointed out that a pandemic on the scale of COVID-19 was uninsurable. As one insurer explained to us: "this is too big for the industry. In other words, it's just a government issue. The industry has no part to play" (Interview—Insurance Industry).

Pandemic is a much faster-moving and more immediate type of systemic risk than climate change.[28] Nonetheless, it provides an important indicator of the limitations that the global insurance system faces in a world where increasingly frequent, severe, and concurrent disasters contribute to a growing problem of uninsurability.

Traditional private-sector insurance is mostly under industry control, with government control limited to setting some broad "rules of the game." This is because, by working well as a market, insurance mostly satisfies society's expectations of protection from loss. However, the inability of the industry to deal with the challenges of disaster insurance creates a social problem.[29] This problem—the loss of financial protection from disaster—is no longer a dystopian future but an increasingly urgent present. To ensure ongoing protection from disaster, insurance *has* to be reimagined. Here, PGEs have a role to play.

6.3 PGEs at the nexus of local and global insurance systems

Our book has examined PGEs as ad hoc local interventions initiated by governments to increase insurability in the face of disasters, with the aim of protecting more members of their society. As shown in the previous chapters, these local efforts point to numerous non-traditional ways in which insurance can be reimagined for the greater benefit of society.[30] For example, by overriding knowledge deficits (Chapter 2); enforcing solidarity as a means of protecting high-risk individuals (Chapter 3); evolving to address new areas of disaster (Chapter 4); and providing some stimulus to increase resilience (Chapter 5). Hence, as more properties are becoming uninsurable in the private sector, existing PGEs are being called upon to fulfill more functions and new PGEs are established. For example, during the research for this book: a cyclone reinsurance pool was established in Australia; wildfire insurance came under the remit of the California Earthquake Authority (CEA); the African Risk Capacity (ARC) began to provide excess rainfall products to African countries; and the South-East Asian Disaster Risk Insurance Facility (SEADRIF) began offering its first flood insurance product in Lao PDR. We argue that PGEs can no longer be considered as separate from the global insurance system, developed to address some local anomaly that makes risk uninsurable in the private market.[31] Rather, PGEs are here to stay; integral to the process of making disaster insurable at the local and global level in the age of climate change.

6.3.1 Effects at the local level

In this book, we have explained how PGEs mitigate the effects of disequilibrium locally. They work around the imbalance in the knowledge, control, and responsibility paradoxes in their local contexts to generate insurability in different ways. For example, in Chapter 2 we show how PGEs, such as Flood Re or Caisse Centrale de Réassurance (CCR), can choose to ignore the problem of too much knowledge when pricing risk, to provide a socially oriented, collective approach to insurance. Alternatively, they can work to develop better knowledge, as with the multi-country (e.g., ARC) or the terrorism PGEs (e.g., Pool Re), enabling otherwise uninsurable risk to be at least partially transferred into the private market. In Chapters 3 and 4, we demonstrate that PGEs can create a new equilibrium in many different ways by adopting different positions among the three paradoxes and adjusting these positions according to the changing demands upon them. These differences reflect the demands of their specific local context and have different implications for the extent to which the PGE can address the protection gap. For example, some, such as CEA (see Chapter 2), struggle to increase the take up of insurance, while others, like the Swiss system (see Chapter 5), are even able to have effects upon the wider ecosystem for resilience.

6.3.2 Effects at the global level

In addition to their local effects, PGEs enable these risks to become part of the global insurance market. First, many of them transfer a portion of the local risk that they cover into the global reinsurance market (see Appendix A).

Second, PGEs may act locally but they exchange knowledge with each other through a range of international forums. Examples include the annual International Federation of Terrorism Risk (Re)Insurance Pools (IFTRIP) conference, the World Forum of Catastrophe Programs meetings, and various OECD and World Bank events. These forums provide opportunities for PGE managers to come together to discuss their challenges in working with the uninsurable aspects of extreme weather and seismological disasters and terrorist attacks. Third, as most PGEs are heavily scrutinized through legislative review and external policy evaluations, their lessons, including the criticisms of them, are made easily available to others. For example, the 2010/2011 Christchurch earthquakes in New Zealand provided a sudden and profound test of a PGE. Many PGEs, observing the problems the EQC experienced in settling claims post-disaster, re-examined their own potential for rapid claims handling (Observation fieldnote). Thus, what is experienced or learned by one PGE, while not necessarily directly transferrable into another PGE, is nonetheless the basis for another to develop its own approach to local risk. In this way PGEs provide a platform for broad exchanges between local contexts and the wider global system for working with otherwise uninsurable risk.

In summary, PGEs mitigate the disequilibrium of uninsurability through local actions to make risk insurable. By transferring some of that risk to the global market, and through knowledge exchange between them, they also help to shape the global system for dealing with uninsurable risk. However, much of this is done on an ad hoc basis in response to local problems, rather than as part of a purposive effort to reimagine a disaster insurance system that has, at its heart, a mission to increase societal protection from disaster.

6.4 Toward a new equilibrium: Integrating PGEs in the global insurance system

PGEs are organizations that have created insurability out of uninsurability in collaboration with many different stakeholders, often over decades. They have done so in the context of a large array of different disasters.[32] Over time they have amassed substantial knowledge, relationships, and capabilities that can help address the growing threat of uninsurable risk globally. *Extending and integrating the work of PGEs is central to reimagining a new landscape within which disaster insurance remains possible.*

To make more use of these organizations at the interface between different public, private, and societal stakeholders, it is necessary to consider how their work can generate a new dynamic equilibrium in the underlying knowledge, control, and responsibility paradoxes within which disaster risk is insured. We now consider the interrelated ways in which PGEs' work with these paradoxes can be scaled and further enhanced to reimagine insurance as a system of societal protection from disaster.

6.4.1 Addressing the knowledge (and responsibility) paradox: Linking financial to physical resilience

Disaster insurance sits at the crux of a knowledge problem. There is growing certainty over the increasing frequency and severity of disasters for parts of the population. At the same time, there remains considerable uncertainty over what, specifically, this increase in frequency and severity will mean in terms of losses, and in what time frame.[33] The risk associated with climate change is both too knowable—it will happen—and yet too unknowable[34]— it cannot be modeled with sufficient certainty to price—creating a profound imbalance in the knowledge paradox at the heart of insurance (Chapter 1).[35] Any reimagined insurance system must address this imbalance. As discussed in this book, PGEs are instrumental in finding ways to rebalance the knowledge paradox, by ignoring either the absence or the excess of knowledge; for instance, subsidizing insurance to those for whom the risk of disaster is too certain to be privately insured (see Chapters 2 and 3).

Addressing the knowledge problem by simply ignoring it is not sustainable in the context of climate change. Subsidizing the premiums of high-risk individuals means that their risk of loss is transferred at a rate below its actual cost to the collective.[36] In the short term, the collective pool of premiums can support recovery for those at high-risk. However, as the group of individuals at risk keeps growing, this approach is unsustainable. It is, therefore, essential to use knowledge to promote changes in physical resilience to disaster, so helping to contain losses to both individuals and the collective.[37] Addressing the knowledge paradox will, thus, also address elements of the responsibility paradox, by supporting both financial and physical resilience to disaster (Chapter 5).

Integrating the financial resilience role of PGEs within the wider physical resilience landscape is critical for reimagining insurance. Such integration might hint at some future state in which all properties, having been made resilient to disaster, are fully insurable within a private market. That it is possible to use physical resilience to resolve the knowledge paradox, returning risk to that sweet spot where enough is known about it to calculate a price at which individuals can purchase an affordable premium in a private-sector insurance market (see Chapters 1 and 2). While this might be a theoretical possibility, it is utopian. Rather, we need to manage our expectations.

First, uncertainty abounds over precisely which mitigation measures will have exactly what effects on insurance pricing. For example, in 2019 we attended a conference where the plight of apartment owners in Wellington, New Zealand, was discussed in relation to building code updates. Many stakeholders (from the property owners to the government) were frustrated and surprised that this expensive work that had supposedly reduced earthquake risk had not resulted in more affordable or accessible insurance. Thus, even with focused efforts on physical resilience, some volatility and uncertainty over insurability will remain, for which a PGE is a relevant financial partner.

Second, there will be properties for which, no matter what mitigation measures are taken, the risk of disaster will remain too high. For example, an apartment complex that sits on an earthquake faultline or on the coastline of a hurricane-prone area. These properties, particularly where there are many of them, pose a substantial problem. For some societies, it will be impossible to buy out everybody at risk of disaster and relocate them all to more disaster-resilient properties at speed. Thus, we need to understand that efforts to improve physical resilience will not resolve every protection gap and in full. There will be housing stock that may not be long-term insurable, and will not be able to be sold, but will, nonetheless, remain inhabited for some time.

Here PGEs might be able to help by offering some support during a period of transition.

Third, contradictions across different stakeholders can make resilience difficult. For example, our opening vignette showed that, within days of the flooding in Australia, state government planning permissions focused on building affordable housing, dismissing concerns for flood resilience. Yet the federal disaster agency had recommended *not* rebuilding housing in disaster-prone areas. The problem is that affordable housing and flood-resilient housing are both important and often contradictory priorities according to politicians' different portfolios, and at different levels of government. Integration of physical and financial resilience will be a complex, tension-laden, multi-stakeholder issue that requires constant work rather than a final end-point that resolves the problem once and for all. PGEs can be a helpful player in navigating these contradictions. As shown throughout this book, PGEs have capabilities in working with the different political demands upon them and the different priorities that need to be met to ensure that a market system can continue to fulfill a societal need for protection. PGEs are thus well-placed to facilitate links between all the stakeholders—insurers, government agencies, construction companies, and planners to name a few—in the ongoing and deepening relationship between resilience and insurance. To do so, they will need to be integrated within the resilience ecosystem of their national and regional contexts and be empowered to play a part in ensuring progress toward physical resilience to disaster.

In summary, PGEs can play a key role in reimaging the insurance landscape by helping to build physical resilience to disaster. There is no utopian future in which all disaster risks can be known, mitigated, and returned to the private sector. PGEs will, nonetheless, be able to support individuals to remain insured and to be more responsible members of an insured collective. The PGE role may include:

- Paying claims that enable disaster-prone building stock to be rebuilt to more resilient specifications (e.g., Flood Re and CEA), so enabling those individuals to access more affordable insurance;
- Funding research and education on disasters and ways of reducing their effect, socially and economically (e.g., ARC, CCRIF, and EQC);
- Using the knowledge that they have access to, or that they develop, to build data and modeling and make these available to inform decisions about physical resilience (e.g., ARPC, Pool Re, Consorcio, and the Swiss system);
- Being integrated into their national and regional disaster resilience landscape in ways that enable insurance information to inform current

and future building permissions and relocations (e.g., Swiss system and CCR);

- Negotiating amongst stakeholders' contradictory priorities whilst keeping the focus on evolving to respond to increasing risk (e.g., ARPC, Flood Re, Consorcio).

Some of these activities are done sporadically, or in different ways in different contexts by different PGEs. Some PGEs are at the forefront in this effort, and some play a smaller role. However, as our study progressed, we have seen most PGEs become significantly more active in resilience, and actively attempting to learn from each other in this area. This is an encouraging sign. Nonetheless, much remains to be done.

6.4.2 Addressing the control paradox: Government and private-sector collaboration

The control paradox—who controls the insurance market—is also central in reimagining insurance. While the insurance market is typically run by the insurance industry, which needs to be profitable, the government needs to retain some control to ensure that insurance provides a societally acceptable level of disaster protection. Breakdowns in disaster protection have led to the formation of many PGEs, often raising tensions between governments and the insurance industry about who should control the market.

A reimagined insurance system must reconceive the control paradox in the context of disaster insurance: governments must intervene in the market and the industry must collaborate and support those interventions. This does not mean that governments should fully underwrite the market, providing an unlimited capital guarantee. Neither does it mean that the private sector should have no or a smaller role in insurance. Indeed, it will remain critical. Rather, it means generating a new dynamic equilibrium that meets the demands of a world affected by forces such as the climate crisis, increasing urbanization, and geopolitical instability—an equilibrium in which PGEs are considered part of the global insurance landscape rather than an anomaly within it.

Many of the PGEs formed in the last three decades are viewed as "temporary" solutions, needed only to address moments of private-sector failure, and tightly bound around a specific gap in the market. Yet, as the previous chapters show, insurance is often only brought about and continues because of the PGEs that sit between the needs of the government and the private industry. It is not clear that PGEs can be eliminated. Where efforts at doing so have been made, most prominently in the case of TRIA (see Chapter 1, Case 1.1), they have failed. PGEs often enable the profitability of the insurance industry to continue in many areas of risk, even as they secure and expand protection for policyholders. They can, therefore, be considered as part of the system, rather than a less-than-ideal anomaly or a stopgap.

While not yet widespread, there are indications that the concept of PGEs as government, industry, and wider stakeholder collaborations to expand insurance, is indeed widening. Innovations show the increasing scale of the PGE concept, as new forms of public, private, NGO, and civil society collaboration emerge to insure what would otherwise be uninsurable risk, as per the example of the Mesoamerican Reef Insurance Program (Case 6.1).

Case example 6.1: Mesoamerican Reef Insurance Program: Expanding the PGE concept to natural assets

As extreme weather wreaks havoc on natural assets like coral reefs, insurance is one proposed source of capital to repair these assets after disasters such as hurricanes.

One example is the Mesoamerican Reef Insurance Program, established in 2019 through a collaboration between the Nature Conservancy NGO, a Mexican state government, the tourism industry operating in the area, scientists, and the international insurance industry. This program initially provided disaster liquidity insurance to cover 160 km of the Mesoamerican barrier reef. Following Hurricane Delta in 2020, an insurance payout of $1.14 million allowed swift damage assessments, debris removal, and initial repairs to the reef, alongside preparation for restoration and recovery work. This enabled rapid response to prevent further deterioration, ensuring that coastlines would continue to be protected by the reef, and that the reef itself would remain an important and viable resource for tourism revenue. As Fernando Secaira of The Nature Conservancy noted: "this innovative approach to protecting reefs paid off. Insurance plus government commitments paired with on-the-ground rapid response create the perfect formula to quickly repair critical coral reefs. It's a win-win and we look forward to identifying other parts of the world where this approach could work."* For the global insurance industry, it was also positive as it was one more area of risk on which to use their capital, albeit not one they could easily have brought to market by themselves.

In 2021 this program was extended to three more countries, with the aim to eventually insure the full 1,000 km of the Mesoamerican barrier reef.

---

* Winters, R., "World's First Coral Reef Insurance Policy Triggered by Hurricane Delta." *The Nature Conservancy*, December 7, 2020. Available from: https://www.nature.org/en-us/newsroom/coral-reef-insurance-policy-triggered/

Other innovations are emerging from a range of different collaborations.[38] For example, donor-led efforts, such as the German development agency InsuResilience, and humanitarian efforts, such as the World Food Program and Start Network, are building insurance into anticipatory financing for post-disaster relief efforts. Previously, humanitarian disaster response was funded by charitable giving, donors, and development agencies. Insurance is now an additional source of anticipatory financing for humanitarian disaster response, for example, enabling humanitarian agencies to buy a disaster liquidity insurance product for a specific country through a PGE, such as African Risk Capacity (see Chapter 4, Case 4.1). The premium to buy these products is funded by donors and underwritten by the private insurance industry. And the products trigger at a contractually agreed point in a disaster—such as the onset of a drought—releasing cash immediately for the humanitarian response. Such initiatives harness the power of insurance to ensure cash for humanitarian relief is in place prior to the disaster, rather than a mad scramble to find it afterwards. By leveraging private capital, these initiatives can enable donor funds to go further, whilst also expanding opportunities for the insurance industry. In other initiatives, the private industry is embracing the turn to collaboration, such as the Insurance Development Forum, a private-sector-initiated effort to work with governments, development banks, and NGOs on novel ways to insure disasters.

Table 6.1 provides a brief, rather than exhaustive, overview of the various types of initiatives emerging that constitute an expansion of the PGE concept. Our point is that it is necessary to consider PGEs, both in their current forms discussed in this book and these burgeoning new forms of collaboration, as central parties in a reimagined global insurance system. This new landscape will continue to experience tensions over control, as it will be imperfect and evolving. However, stakeholders will be comfortable with working with the contradictions that public-private collaboration entails, as part of the ongoing quest to improve physical and financial resilience to disasters.

6.4.3 Addressing the responsibility paradox: Should insurance be mandatory?

A reimagined insurance landscape relies on available, affordable, and sustainable disaster insurance for the protection of society. In a world of increasing disaster, private-sector disaster insurance faces severe challenges and, potentially, the risk of breakdown. PGEs have come about at these points of breakdown, providing insights into how insurance markets of the future will have to address the issue of *who is responsible for disaster protection*. As our

Table 6.1 Growth in the wider PGE concept.

Example of Initiative	Key characteristics
Donor initiatives: e.g., InsuResilience;[a] Global Risk Financing Facility (GRIF)[b]	Donor-led initiatives to support provision of insurance as part of development, climate, and humanitarian relief. These initiatives provide a range of support from financing the technical and operating capabilities of PGEs, such as ARC, to premium support, in conjunction with other donor countries and the World Bank.
Humanitarian initiatives: e.g., Start Network;[c] World Food Program[d]	Humanitarian initiatives to stabilize their post-disaster funding capabilities through the purchase of insurance products. These products provide a payout that enables humanitarian agencies to provide a rapid response to alleviate the effects of disasters within countries.
Private industry initiatives: e.g., Insurance Development Forum;[e] Blue Marble[f]	Private industry initiatives, usually comprising a consortium of insurance companies coming together to provide market capital and technical support for social insurance projects. These are focused on addressing risks that would otherwise be underserved or not served at all by insurance capital. These initiatives, which often expand to become cross-sector, can provide the technical assistance to develop a product and source the market capital for it.
Problem-led initiatives: e.g., Mesoamerican Reef Insurance Program;[g] CCRIF[h]	Initiatives where a problem that would not usually attract an insurance response brings collaborators together to model risk, develop products, source premium providers, and insurance market capital to offer protection. These initiatives can become institutionalized over time. For example, the Caribbean Catastrophe Risk Insurance Facility (CCRIF) began as a novel problem-led initiative by the Caribbean Community following Hurricane Ivan in 2004.

a. InsuResilience. Date accessed: September 2022. Available from: https://www.insuresilience.org/
b. Global Risk Financing Facility. Date accessed: September 2022. Available from: https://globalriskfinancing.org/
c. Start Network. Date accessed: September 2022. Available from: https://startnetwork.org/
d. World Food Program. Date accessed: September 2022. Available from: https://www.wfp.org/
e. Insurance Development Forum. Date accessed: September 2022. Available from: https://www.insdevforum.org
f. Blue Marble. Date accessed: September 2022. Available from: https://bluemarblemicro.com
g. MAR Fund. Date accessed: September 2022. Available from: https://marfund.org/en/
h. CCRIF. Date accessed: September 2022. Available from: https://www.ccrif.org/

analysis has shown, those PGEs set up to emphasize individual responsibility for protection, typically through risk-reflective pricing, and to bolster industry control over insurance markets, have comparatively little impact on ensuring widespread insurance protection from disaster (see Chapters 3 and 4). It thus seems inevitable that protecting individuals from disaster will require more collectivization of risk than many are used to.

We agree that, in principle, individuals need to be responsible for containing their losses from disasters to prevent an undue burden on society.

However, for individuals to be able to take responsibility, they must start from a position in which their properties are not disproportionately vulnerable to disaster.[39] That is, they must already have been moved from the flood plains or have had their homes built to withstand hurricanes. To ensure a more level playing field for individuals to act responsibly in containing loss, therefore, strong government-level investments in physical as well as financial resilience are needed. As we have discussed (see Chapter 5 and section 6.4.1), with an appropriate mandate, PGEs can be an important vehicle for this integration of physical and financial resilience to take place. Such integration reduces the burden to the collective of excessive loss from some individuals.

PGEs are particularly effective vehicles for instigating collective responsibility for disaster, because, with government intervention, they can spread the risk of multiple types of disasters across all members of a society (see Chapters 2 and 3). However, to further a collective approach to protection, PGEs will have to grapple with what is often a thorny problem for societies with a strong culture of marketization and a strong focus on individual responsibility; *should disaster insurance be mandatory*? By mandatory disaster insurance we mean that individuals are required to buy, and the insurance market must offer, disaster insurance. In a reimagined insurance landscape, disaster insurance will, most likely, only be possible when it is made mandatory. This is because mandatory insurance ensures that a wide protection net is spread across society, encompassing all individuals within a collective responsibility for protection.[40] Mandatory schemes are already a feature of some areas of insurance. For example, compulsory third-party (CTP) motor vehicle insurance is widely accepted as part of car insurance in many countries. This insurance, often a condition of registering a vehicle, provides protection for people who may be injured or killed in a motor vehicle accident. Effectively, this CTP motor insurance means that every vehicle owner must buy the insurance and makes the entire vehicle-owning population of a country into a collective with responsibility to pay for extreme losses to any individual. In those countries that already have mandatory insurance for some disasters (such as New Zealand, France, and Spain), disaster insurance is often coupled with the general insurance purchase. For example, earthquake insurance is mandatory as part of fire insurance in New Zealand (via the Earthquake Commission—EQC). In these contexts of heightened government control of the insurance market, the PGE's role is to ensure the affordability of this mandatory insurance. In tandem with the integration of insurance with physical resilience, and active collaboration between government and the insurance industry, mandatory insurance via PGEs is one way to reimagine responsibility for insurance protection. Hence, despite the difficulties of setting up and running mandatory systems effectively, they seem our best option to achieve affordable and sustainable insurance. Drawing inspiration from Churchill, mandatory schemes are "the worst form" of disaster protection "except for all those other forms that have been tried from time to time."[41] Mandatory insurance can indeed work as a means of rebalancing the responsibility paradox, where it is fully integrated within a new equilibrium of physical and financial resilience and collaborative control over the insurance market; in effect in a reimagined insurance landscape.

6.5 Conclusion: Reimagining insurance in an ecosystem of protection

We have argued for a new dynamic equilibrium in which PGEs, in both their existing forms and in the burgeoning expansions of the PGE concept, are integral to the global insurance system. Our strong advocacy for PGEs is not because they are a silver bullet to save private-sector disaster insurance from obsolescence. Rather, in a world of increasing disaster, it is essential to recalibrate the entire ecosystem for disaster protection. Insurance will be one key part of that new ecosystem. Based on our extensive fieldwork, we offer a vision for how to reimagine insurance within the ecosystem of protection: embracing knowledge to build stronger links between physical and financial resilience; acknowledging government and industry collaboration in insurance markets; and accepting that collective responsibility for protection will be necessary to enable individuals to act responsibly in their own protection. PGEs, with their expertise, political capabilities, and role at the intersection of many of the stakeholders in the insurance and resilience landscape, provide one vehicle to create our vision of an ecosystem of protection. This ecosystem would have societal protection from disaster at its heart, with insurance, reimagined, as an effective tool for protection.

Notes

1. Australian Disaster Resilience Knowledge Hub, *Queensland and Brisbane 2010/11 Floods.* Canberra: Australian Government, National Emergency Management Agency, 2012. Available from: https://knowledge.aidr.org.au/resources/flood-queensland-2010-2011/
2. Brewster, A., "South-East Queensland's Floods were Labelled a 'Once-in-100-Year' Event, So What does that Actually Mean?" *ABC News,* March 20, 2022. Available from: https://www.abc.net.au/news/2022-03-21/qld-what-is-a-once-in-100-year-flood-weather-event/100917578

3. Yeates, C., "Home Insurance Premiums Tipped to Jump More than 10% after Floods." *Sydney Morning Herald,* March 9, 2022. Available from: https://www.smh.com.au/business/banking-and-finance/home-insurance-premiums-tipped-to-jump-more-than-10-after-floods-20220309-p5a348.html.

   Walsh, L., "Wave of Disasters Forcing 'Double-Digit' Insurance Premium Rises." *Financial Review,* March 17, 2022. Available from: https://www.afr.com/companies/financial-services/wave-of-disasters-forcing-double-digit-insurance-premium-rises-20220316-p5a59z

4. Insurance News, "Shallow Solution: Do Floods Expose Pool Limitations?" March 14, 2022. Available from: https://www.insurancenews.com.au/analysis/shallow-solution-do-floods-expose-pool-limitations

5. Power, J., "NSW Planning Minister Scraps Order to Consider Flood, Fire Risks before Building." *Sydney Morning Herald,* March 22, 2022. Available from: https://www.smh.com.au/national/nsw/nsw-planning-minister-scraps-order-to-consider-flood-fire-risks-before-building-20220321-p5a6kc.html

6. Lefebvre, M., Reinard, J., *The Cost of Extreme Weather: Building Resilience in the Face of Disaster.* Sydney: McKell Institute, September 2022. Available from https://insurancecouncil.com.au/wp-content/uploads/2022/09/McKell_Cost-of-Natural-Disasters_SINGLES_WEB.pdf

7. Insurance News,. "Flood Losses Reach $5.45 Billion, Over Half Claims Closed: ICA." September 30, 2022. Available from: https://www.insurancenews.com.au/daily/flood-losses-reach-5-45-billion-over-half-claims-closed-ica

8. Perils, "AUD 4,895m—Perils Discloses Second Loss Estimate for Eastern Australia Floods of February–March 2022." Press release, June 9, 2022. Available from: https://www.perils.org/news/aud-4-895m-perils-releases-second-industry-loss-estimate-for-the-eastern-australia-floods-of-february-march-2022

9. Cal Fire, 2020 and 2021 incident archives. State of California, 2020 and 2021. Available from: https://www.fire.ca.gov/incidents/2020/ and https://www.fire.ca.gov/incidents/2021/

10. Routley, N., "5 Things to Know about Europe's Scorching Heatwave." World Economic Forum, July 21, 2022. Available from: https://www.weforum.org/agenda/2022/07/heatwaves-europe-climate-change/

11. Ellerbeck, S., "The Horn of Africa is Facing an Unprecedented Drought. What is the World Doing to Help Solve it?" World Economic Forum, July 21, 2022. Available from: https://www.weforum.org/agenda/2022/07/africa-drought-food-starvation/

12. Hecht, S. B., "Climate Change and the Transformation of Risk: Insurance Matters." *UCLA Law Review,* 55(6) (2007): 1559–1620.

13. Jarzabkowski, P., Bednarek, R., Spee, P., *Making a Market for Acts of God: The Practice of Risk-Trading in the Global Reinsurance Industry.* New York: Oxford University Press, 2015.

   Grant, E., *The Social and Economic Value of Insurance.* Geneva: Geneva Association, 2012. Available from: https://www.genevaassociation.org/sites/default/files/research-topics-document-type/pdf_public//ga2012-the_social_and_economic_value_of_insurance.pdf

14. Carpenter, O., Platt, S., Evan, T., Mahdavian, F., Coburn, A., *Optimising Disaster Recovery: The Role of Insurance Capital in Improving Economic Resilience.* Cambridge: AXA

and Centre for Risk Studies at the University of Cambridge, Judge, 2020. Available from: https://axaxl.com/-/media/axaxl/files/optimizing-disaster-recovery.pdf

15. Carpenter et al., *Optimising Disaster R*

16. De Vet, E., Eriksen, C., Booth, K., French, S., "An Unmitigated Disaster: Shifting from Response and Recovery to Mitigation for an Insurable Future." *International Journal of Disaster Risk Science*, 10(2) (2019): 179–92. https://doi.org/10.1007/s13753-019-0214-0.

    Lucas, C. H., Booth, K. I., "Privatizing Climate Adaptation: How Insurance Weakens Solidaristic and Collective Disaster Recovery." *Wiley Interdisciplinary Reviews: Climate Change*, 11(6) (2020): e676. https://doi.org/10.1002/wcc.676.

    Elliott, R., *Underwater: Loss, Flood Insurance, and the Moral Economy of Climate Change in the United States*. New York: Columbia University Press, 2021.

17. Outreville, J. F., "The Relationship between Insurance and Economic Development: 85 Empirical Papers for a Review of the Literature." *Risk Management and Insurance Review*, 16(1) (2013): 71–122. https://doi.org/10.1111/j.1540-6296.2012.01219.x

18. Ranger, N., Mahul, O., Monasterolo, I., "Managing the Financial Risks of Climate Change and Pandemics: What we Know (and Don't Know)." *One Earth*, 4(10) (2021): 1375–85. https://doi.org/10.1016/j.oneear.2021.09.017

19. Hill, A. C., Martinez-Diaz, L., *Building a Resilient Tomorrow: How to Prepare for the Coming Climate Disruption*. New York: Oxford University Press, 2020.

20. Pörtner, H.-O., Roberts, D. C., Tignor, M., Poloczanska, E. S., Mintenbeck, K., Alegría, A., Craig, M., Langsdorf, S., Löschke, S., Möller, V., Okem, A., Rama, B., eds, *Climate Change 2022: Impacts, Adaptation and Vulnerability*. IPCC. Contribution of working group II to the sixth assessment report of the intergovernmental panel on climate change. Cambridge: Cambridge University Press, 2022, 1–3. Available from: https://www.ipcc.ch/report/ar6/wg2/downloads/report/IPCC_AR6_WGII_FullReport.pdf

21. Owen, S., Noy, I., "Regressivity in Public Natural Hazard Insurance: A Quantitative Analysis of the New Zealand Case." *Economics of Disasters and Climate Change*, 3(3) (2019): 235–55. https://doi.org/10.1007/s41885-019-00043-1.

    Kunreuther, H., Pauly, M., "Insuring Against Catastrophes." In: Diebold, F. X., Doherty, N. A., Herring, R. J., eds, *The Known, the Unknown, and the Unknowable in Financial Risk Management: Measurement and Theory Advancing Practice*. Princeton: Princeton University Press, 2010, chapter 10.

22. Haueter, N. V., *A History of Insurance*. Zurich: Swiss Re, 2013. Available from: https://www.swissre.com/dam/jcr:638f00a0-71b9-4d8e-a960-dddaf9ba57cb/150_history_of_insurance.pdf

23. Douris, J., Kim, G., *WMO Atlas of Mortality and Economic Losses from Weather, Climate and Water Extremes (1970–2019)*. Geneva: World Meteorological Organization, 2021. Available from: https://library.wmo.int/index.php?lvl=notice_display&id=21930#.Yz72fHbMKUk.

    Pörtner et al., *Climate Change 2022*. Ranger et al., "Managing the Financial Risks."

24. Golnaraghi, M., *Climate Change Risk Assessment for the Insurance Industry*. Geneva: Geneva Association, 2021. Available from: https://www.genevaassociation.org/publication/climate-change-and-environment/climate-change-risk-assessment-insurance-industry.

Ross, H., *Climate Risks for Insurers: Why the Industry Needs to Act Now to Address Climate Risk on Both Sides of the Balance Sheet*. S&P Global, August 27, 2021. Available from: https://www.spglobal.com/esg/insights/climate-risks-for-insurers-why-the-industry-needs-to-act-now-to-address-climate-risk-on-both-sides-of-the-balance-sheet.

Bachir, M., Gokhale, N., Ashani, P., *Climate Risk: Regulators Sharpen their Focus*. London: Deloitte, 2019. Available from: https://www.deloitte.com/us/en/pages/financial-services/articles/insurance-companies-climate-change-risk.html.

Guo, J., Kubli, D., Saner, P., *The Economics of Climate Change: No Action Not an Option*. Zurich: Swiss Re, 2021. Available from: https://www.swissre.com/institute/research/topics-and-risk-dialogues/climate-and-natural-catastrophe-risk/expertise-publication-economics-of-climate-change.html.

Aon, *2021 Weather, Climate and Catastrophe Insight*. London: AON, 2022. Available from: https://www.aon.com/weather-climate-catastrophe/index.html

25. Ranger et al., "Managing the Financial Risks.".

Schanz, K. U., Jarzabkowski, P., Cacciatori, E., Chalkias, K., Kavas, M., Krull, E., *Public-Private Solutions to Pandemic Risk: Opportunities, Challenges and Trade-offs*. Zurich: Geneva Association, 2021. Available from: https://www.genevaassociation.org/sites/default/files/research-topics-document-type/pdf_public/pandemic_solutions-report_final.pdf

26. Clissitt, M., *Systemic Risk and the Insurance Sector*. London: Chartered Insurance Institute, 2021. Available from: https://www.cii.co.uk/media/10127435/cii-systemic-risk-report.pdf

27. Ralph, O., "Insurers Braced for Claims from Covid-19 Legal Action." *Financial Times*, April 6, 2020. Available from: https://www.ft.com/content/2d388a77-8706-4387-85b7-09c7bd16a0a8.

Croft, J., "Collective Legal Actions Spread in Europe." *Financial Times*, October 15, 2021. Available from: https://www.ft.com/content/1f2585e0-eb02-4d04-80a8-1797bf739f21

28. Boin, A., Ekengren, M., Rhinard, M., "Hiding in Plain Sight: Conceptualizing the Creeping Crisis." *Risk, Hazards and Crisis in Public Policy*, 11(2) (2020): 116–38. https://doi.org/10.1002/rhc3.12193.

Unger, C., *Insidious Risk Management: A Practice Theoretical Perspective*. Brisbane: UQ Business School, University of Queensland, 2021. https://doi.org/10.14264/2393daa

29. Klein, K. S., "Is Fire Insurable?: Insights from Bushfires in Australia and Wildfires in the United States." In Booth, K., Lucas, C., French, S., eds, *Climate, Society and Elemental Insurance: Capacities and Limitations*. Abingdon: Routledge, 2022, 111–24.

30. Ewald, F., "Insurance and Risk." In Burchell, G., Gordon, C., Miller, P., eds, *The Foucault Effect: Studies in Governmentality*. Chicago: University of Chicago Press, 1991, 197–210.

Collier, S. J., Elliott, R., Lehtonen, T.-K., "Climate Change and Insurance." *Economy and Society*, 50(2) (2021): 158–72. https://doi.org/10.1080/03085147.2021.1903771

31. Christophers, B., "The Allusive Market: Insurance of Flood Risk in Neoliberal Britain." *Economy and Society*, 48(1) (2019): 1–29. https://doi.org/10.1080/03085147.2018.1547494

32. Kousky, C. *Understanding Disaster Insurance: New Tools for a More Resilient Future*. Washington, DC: Island Press, 2022.

   Kunreuther, H., "The Role of Insurance in Reducing Losses from Extreme Events: The Need for Public-Private Partnerships." *The Geneva Papers on Risk and Insurance—Issues and Practice*, 40 (2015): 741–62. https://doi.org/10.1057/gpp.2015.14

33. Emanuel, K., *What we Know about Climate Change*. Cambridge, MA: MIT Press, 2018.

34. Beck, U., "The Terrorist Threat: World Risk Society Revisited." *Theory, Culture and Society*, 19(4) (2002): 39–55. https://doi.org/10.1177/0263276402019004003

35. Gray, I., "Hazardous Simulations: Pricing Climate Risk in US Coastal Insurance Markets." *Economy and Society*, 50(2) (2021): 196–223. https://doi.org/10.1080/03085147.2020.1853358

36. Elliott, *Underwater*.

37. Kunreuther, "Role of Insurance." https://doi.org/10.1057/gpp.2015.14.

   Nussbaum, R., "Involving Public Private Partnerships as Building Blocks For Integrated Natural Catastrophes Country Risk Management-Sharing on the French National Experiences of Economic Instruments Integrated with Information and Knowledge Management Tools." *IDRiM Journal*, 5(2) (2015): 82–100. https://doi.org/10.5595/idrim.2015.0116

38. Kousky, *Understanding Disaster Insurance*.

39. Elliott, *Underwater*.

   Hutter, B. M., ed., *Risk, Resilience, Inequality and Environmental Law*. Cheltenham: Edward Elgar Publishing, 2017, 207–27.

   Knighton, J., Hondula, K., Sharkus, C., Guzman, C., Elliott, R., "Flood Risk Behaviors of United States Riverine Metropolitan Areas are Driven by Local Hydrology and Shaped by Race." *Proceedings of the National Academy of Sciences*, 118(13) (2021): e2016839118. https://doi.org/10.1073/pnas.2016839118

40. Kunreuther, H., Pauly, M., "Rules rather than Discretion: Lessons from Hurricane Katrina." *Journal of Risk and Uncertainty*, 33(1) (2006): 101–16. https://doi.org/10.1007/s11166-006-0173-x Kunreuther, "Role of Insurance."

41. Churchill, W., *Quotes*. International Churchill Society. Date accessed: September 2022. Available from: https://winstonchurchill.org/resources/quotes/the-worst-form-of-government/

The disaster risk transfer process

1. The traditional (re)insurance market

The purpose of disaster insurance is to transfer the risk of loss from a disaster, such as a major flood or hurricane, from insured *individuals and businesses* to insurers. This helps these individuals and businesses pay for repairs after a disaster.

Insurers accept the risk from insureds in exchange for a *premium*. Insurers are then responsible to pay for the potential future financial losses arising from disaster according to the terms and conditions of the *insurance policy*. If a loss occurs, insurers will pay *claims* as specified in the insurance policy. For example, individuals can buy an insurance policy to protect their house from flood. They can decide the level of cover (for what proportion of their house value they will buy cover) and how much risk to retain themselves ("excess" or threshold they will pay themselves for damage before their insurance starts to pay). These different factors affect the amount of their premium. Then if a flood damages their house, insurers will issue a payout based on the cover bought through the insurance policy. Insurers calculate and charge premiums, so that the accumulated premiums of the many insureds over time cover the losses of the unfortunate few that suffer losses from disasters. Insurers are typically private-sector companies that make a profit through this risk transfer process.

Insurers must also protect themselves from a disaster that gives them many claims at once. They, therefore, transfer some risk via *reinsurance* to ensure they will remain solvent to pay claims after a big disaster. Essentially, reinsurance is insurance for insurance companies. Each insurer transfers some of their risk to a panel of multiple reinsurers. As with insurance risk transfer, reinsurers agree on the conditions upon which to pay their share of that insurer's *claims*, in return for which they receive a reinsurance *premium*. Reinsurance capital can come from *reinsurers* that accept insurance risk for a profit and other *financial market* providers, such as hedge funds, mutual funds, sovereign wealth funds, pension funds, and institutional investors, also accepting risk for a profit (see Figure A.1).

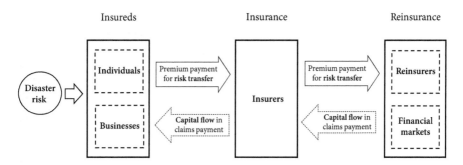

Figure A.1 The risk transfer process in the traditional (re)insurance market.

2. PGE intervention

While the traditional (re)insurance market is critical in assisting individuals and businesses to withstand financial loss after disasters, a significant portion of disaster risk globally is not insured, resulting in an insurance protection gap (see Introduction). The risk transfer process just described is typically a private-sector mechanism. However, when an insurance protection gap arises governments can intervene in the risk transfer process to make at least some of that risk insurable. Such interventions take the form of Protection Gap Entities—PGEs (see Chapter 1). These PGEs adopt different strategies for making risk insurable, which can range from governments taking some risk upon their own balance sheet, to introducing schemes such as publicly funded or privately funded but publicly managed (re)insurance pools, to using developmental and donor funds to subsidize some form of insurance provision for countries. The aim of these PGEs is to introduce, increase, or restore insurability to risk that would otherwise be uninsurable in the private sector.

2.1 PGE position in the risk transfer process

PGEs can occupy one of three archetypal positions in the risk transfer process: insurer, reinsurer, and market capture (see Figure A.2).[1] This position simply explains at what point they participate in transferring risk, rather than explaining any variation in their governance structures (e.g., public, private, partnership), risks covered (e.g., single peril or multi-peril), type of risk solution (e.g., product used), and their funding model (e.g., policyholders' premiums, public or private levy).

The *Insurer PGE* operates in the insurance market by providing insurance policies on a particular disaster that is either no longer covered by the private sector or one for which cover has become unaffordable for those highly exposed to the risk. They provide policies directly to individuals and businesses in return for a premium and are responsible for paying claims.

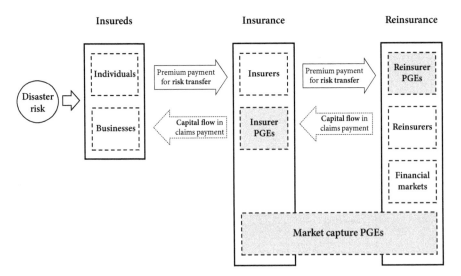

Figure A.2 The risk transfer process after PGEs' intervention (individuals and businesses are the insureds).

They can also buy reinsurance from the private sector to cover their risk exposure. Examples of the Insurer PGE are the NZ Earthquake Commission (EQC), the California Earthquake Authority (CEA), and the USA National Flood Insurance Program (NFIP).

The *Reinsurer PGE* operates as a reinsurance pool. They typically intervene either when there is a supply failure in the private reinsurance sector (e.g., Pool Re or Australian Reinsurance Pool Corporation (ARPC) or when insurance premiums become unaffordable (e.g., Flood Re). They enable the insurance market to continue offering policies by transferring the proportion of risk that would otherwise form an identified protection gap from any insurance policy to a Reinsurer PGE. For example, insurers in the UK can offer flood insurance to individuals, knowing that they can transfer the risk of a loss from flood to the Reinsurer PGE, Flood Re.

The *Market Capture PGE* operates in both the insurance and reinsurance spaces. It acts as an insurer for all, or at least most, disaster risks in a country. They do so either alongside private insurers as an additional product or by "co-insuring" on existing products with the private insurers. Because it typically holds all the risks in a country, the Market Capture PGE has a highly diversified portfolio that enables it to optimize its capital reserves. Thus, it does not necessarily need to purchase reinsurance but can choose instead to act as its own reinsurer. This type of PGE is typically a public-sector organization. An example of the Market Capture PGE is Consorcio in Spain.

2.2 PGE strategies for transferring risk

When they intervene in the traditional risk transfer process, PGEs have two main strategies for transferring risk, removing risk and/or redistributing risk. Some PGEs combine the two strategies.[2]

Removing risk refers to an intervention where a PGE removes risk from the insurance industry onto the PGE or government balance sheet. This is particularly likely for disasters that are seen as too volatile or extreme for the private sector to insure. For example, a PGE may take all the earthquake risk in an area such as California, so that the PGE, not the industry, will pay the claims after an earthquake. It can also focus on removing the most extreme risk that is the most difficult to insure by the private market. For example, a PGE such as ARPC may pay the highest levels of claims arising from a terrorist attack, while the insurers pay the lower-level claims.

Redistributing risk refers to a PGE taking insurance premiums from a group of high-risk policyholders at a lower rate than they would be charged in the private sector. This lower rate is subsidized by redistributing the cost of premiums across all policyholders. Redistribution is typically used in situations where risk-reflective pricing would make insurance unaffordable for policyholders in high-risk areas. A PGE may redistribute the risk by charging a flat rate for disaster insurance across all policyholders at a national level. This is typically supported by the government legislating mandatory disaster insurance. A PGE can also redistribute the risk from a small group of policyholders across all policyholders. This is typically supported by a levy on all other policyholders, who are each charged a small amount more in their premiums to subsidize the reduction in price to the small group that are at high-risk of loss.

2.3 PGE intervention for governments

The PGE strategies explained in 2.2 are relevant to a mature insurance market where the insureds are individuals or businesses. However, there are also protection gaps where the insureds are sovereigns seeking financial protection for the effects of disaster upon the nation

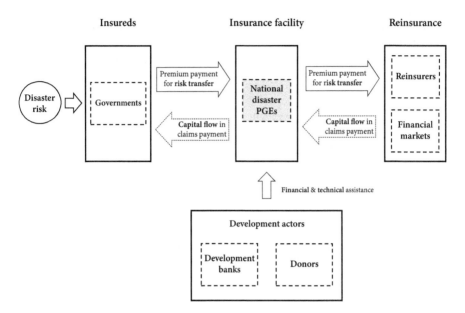

Figure A.3 The risk transfer process after PGEs' intervention (governments are the insureds).

(see Figure A.3). *National Disaster PGEs*[3] are insurance-based facilities to provide governments with parametric insurance products in exchange for a premium.[4] Acting as the insurer to these countries, these PGEs retain some of the disaster risks of the member governments on their balance sheet and then transfer the rest to traditional reinsurers and financial markets. While the structure resembles a traditional insurer, there are two striking differences. First, National Disaster PGEs are not-for-profit organizations that often receive substantial financial and technical assistance from development banks and donors to operate. Second, while private insurers retain a substantial part of the insureds' risk and transfer just some of that to reinsurers, National Disaster PGEs do the opposite. They retain some, typically a small part, of the risk and then transfer most of it to reinsurers which therefore are liable for most of the claims' payments. This type of PGE may be an insurance facility for a single sovereign, such as FONDEN in Mexico, or, increasingly, are multi-country PGEs, such as the African Risk Capacity (ARC), or the Caribbean Catastrophe Risk Insurance Facility (CCRIF).

Notes

1. Jarzabkowski, P., Chalkias, K., Cacciatori, E., Bednarek, R., *Between State and Market: Protection Gap Entities and Catastrophic Risk.* London: Cass Business School, City, University of London, 2018, 12–19: section 3, "In the Presence of a Mature Insurance Market: Market Dynamics." Available from: https://www.bayes.city.ac.uk/__data/assets/pdf_file/0020/420257/PGE-Report-FINAL.pdf
2. Jarzabkowski et al., *Between State and Market*, 12–19.
3. Throughout this book, the National Disaster PGEs that we explain are multi-country PGEs, and so we use the term multi-country PGE within the book text.
4. Jarzabkowski et al., *Between State and Market*, 20–5: section 4, "Protection for Sovereigns: Insurance as a Disaster Liquidity Product."

Methodology

Our research followed a *phenomenon-driven, inductive* approach that was *global, multi-stakeholder*, and *longitudinal* in nature.

The central aim that guided our research was to seek a deeper understanding and offer insights into a focal *phenomenon*—the problem of disaster insurance protection gaps and the solutions brought to addressing this gap by the various Protection Gap Entities (PGEs). Our approach was *inductive* as we did not start with a specific research question but with an interest in understanding how these entities intervened to address specific disaster protection gaps. Our research design, analytical insights, and research questions grew inductively out of a quest to better understand the phenomenon at hand.

The nature of the phenomenon we investigated prompted a *global* research design. Insurance protection gaps are a global phenomenon. Climate change, increased urbanization, and geopolitical instability that are increasing the protection gap are global issues. Many organizations involved, such as the World Bank or some (re)insurance firms, are global organizations, engaged with protection gaps around the world. Also, the lessons learned and solutions implemented locally in one context are often transferred elsewhere within the global insurance system. While other studies have focused on specific PGEs[1] or compare them,[2] our study traced PGEs as a varied global response to a global problem within the complex and interdependent system of insurance, rather than as separate organizations.

Nonetheless, to understand the phenomenon, we also needed to understand the local contexts in which PGEs respond to the protection gap. Each PGE is distinct and embedded in country-specific contexts that shaped both the disaster being addressed and the PGE's approach to it. Understanding the global phenomenon thus also entailed a focus on local solutions. We therefore zoomed in to collect data within countries, focusing on different local solutions and the stakeholders involved. Then we zoomed out to understand the connections and interdependencies among these local solutions.

Given the complexity of the disaster insurance protection gap, which extends beyond the boundaries of any organization or country, and includes the multiple organizations and communities that PGEs must interact with, we took a *multi-stakeholder* approach. We followed many stakeholders with competing interests and objectives across the world, including PGE managers, and the insurance industry, government, and development stakeholders that worked directly upon, or around, the protection gap phenomenon. Some of these stakeholders worked globally, across multiple PGEs, while others acted mainly at the local level of specific PGEs. Consequently, our research design focused on PGEs as the central organizations addressing protection gaps, but was inter-organizational, focusing on the interdependencies between PGEs and their multiple and diverse stakeholders, locally and globally.

Finally, our research was *longitudinal* as our purpose was to understand the global phenomenon over time. Protection gaps, as well as the local responses to them from PGEs and their stakeholders, are not static. This meant we were interested in exploring how PGEs originated as a response to local gaps, how local gaps evolved, and how PGEs responded (or not) to such evolution. While other studies[3] have shown how various PGEs are structured and governed, our study examined the relationship between PGE evolution and protection gap evolution, in an effort to not only explore their past and current state but also understand and anticipate future issues.

Specifics about research design and data collection

We collected interview, observational, and documentary data on 17 PGEs that are collectively addressing protection gaps in 49 countries. These data collection sites include in-depth primary data with 14 PGEs and their stakeholders, and some broader primary data with an additional three PGEs. Some PGEs are multi-country, while other countries have more than one PGE. We also gained passing familiarity with additional PGEs in other countries through our meetings with them and their stakeholders while participating in conferences and workshops. We traveled extensively for data collection (Australia, Belgium, France, Mexico, New Zealand, Russia, South Africa, Spain, Switzerland, the UK, and the USA) which enabled us to immerse ourselves in some of the field contexts. Given the breadth of our study, phone calls and virtual platforms such as Zoom or Skype also allowed us to expand the global reach of our data collection as well as continue our engagement when the pandemic hit. We also made the most of in-person conferences, and visits to London by any of our participants, to arrange face-to-face meetings to get to know people better. This breadth and depth of data enabled us to capture different understandings of the disaster insurance protection gap and variations in the solutions developed by PGEs around the world.

Our research design was multi-stakeholder. We interviewed not only an array of people working within PGEs, but also external stakeholders including people in government (e.g., ministers, treasury departments, environmental agencies, and development departments), the insurance industry (e.g., insurers, reinsurers, brokers, and modelers), and intergovernmental organizations (e.g., the World Bank, the OECD, and humanitarian and aid organizations).

To enhance the global nature of our research design, we captured interdependencies across PGEs and stakeholders in two ways. First, apart from the PGEs and their stakeholders, we also interviewed stakeholders within multinational organizations that operated across those local contexts, such as global (re)insurers, brokers, modelers, development banks, and international aid and donor organizations. These stakeholders had knowledge of the global protection gap and were also associated with some of the local PGEs. For instance, we interviewed a participant who had in the past worked for an international bank, was active in setting up one PGE, and had advised as an external consultant to another PGE during its development. Such engagement across different PGEs was not unusual, demonstrating the interdependencies within our dataset.

Second, we observed and participated in field-configuring events.[4] These included conferences and workshops where many diverse stakeholders gathered to discuss the protection gap, learn from each other, and make connections. For instance, we participated in the International Forum of Terrorism Risk (Re)Insurance Pools (IFTRIP) where managers in terrorism reinsurance pools meet annually to collaborate and exchange experiences in terrorism risk pooling and mitigation. We were often not just attending but actively participating in these events by chairing sessions or presenting results. For instance, we held a panel at the World Bank Understanding Risk conference with PGE managers and government ministers from three of the multi-country PGEs.

Finally, where opportunity presented itself, we also observed specific PGEs as they made decisions and interacted with their stakeholders about their local protection gap. For instance, we observed numerous board meetings of a PGE while it was developing its remit, sat on advisory panels with another PGE, and attended the public communication events run by PGEs for their immediate stakeholders.

Overall, we collected 460 interviews, each lasting between one and two hours, which were transcribed verbatim; conducted 148 observations lasting from one hour to three days, on which we took detailed fieldnotes; and collected 956 documents about our PGEs (Table B.1). Throughout this book, we provide verbatim extracts from these data. We have, however, edited

Table B.1 Types of data (bold text denotes totals of different subcategories of data and participant).

Interviews per type of participant	**PGEs**	**178**
	Market stakeholders	**181**
	Brokers	32
	Modelers	25
	Insurers	44
	Industry Association	24
	Reinsurers & capital markets	42
	Consultants	14
	Non-market stakeholders	**101**
	Government	50
	Intergovernmental organizations	51
Total interviews		**460**
Interviews per type of context	Emerging markets and developing economies	124
	Advanced economies	287
	Global context	49
Total interviews		**460**
Observations per type of meetings attended	PGE-specific meetings	86
	Field-configuring events (of more than 150 individual sessions)	49
	Social events	13
Total observations		**148**
Total documents	956 comprising 23,620 pages	**956**

such extracts where necessary to make technical insurance or disaster terminology accessible to a wider audience or to preserve the anonymity of the source.

We collected longitudinal data to capture how PGEs evolve in response to changes in their environment and in the protection gaps they are addressing. We collected historical and current documents and also conducted retrospective and real-time interviews. During interviews, we asked about the reasons why a PGE was established as well as their efforts to address the changing nature of disasters and their effect on specific protection gaps. For instance, we discussed the changing nature of terrorism risk in most countries, or the increasing severity of floods or tropical storms in other countries, and how these changed existing, or gave rise to new, protection gaps. We also interviewed stakeholders that had been actively engaged in setting up a PGE or being part of prior government or industry inputs. For instance, we interviewed stakeholders that participated in industry working groups which were the prelude to the launch of Flood Re in 2016. In addition, our real-time data collection of interviews and observations over the 60 months we were actively in the field (2016–20) enabled us to explore the dynamic and shifting nature of the phenomenon. For example, in the Caribbean, we engaged in follow-up interviews with key individuals in the aftermath of the 2017 hurricanes. At a global level, we followed the discussions of issues related to the evolving nature of the focal protection gaps by participating in field-level configuring events in different parts of the world over this same 60-month period. From 2020 to 2022, while we were engaged in writing this book, we also kept track of our various PGEs through their websites, press releases, seeing them at virtual field-configuring events, and through occasional follow-up calls, which allowed us to check impressions and monitor ongoing evolution. This longitudinal nature of our data is reflected in the types of questions we have been able to address in this book.

Data analysis

Our innovative analytical process began with iteration between zooming in, zooming between, and zooming out across contexts, stakeholders, and timelines.[5] Zooming in and out are metaphorical terms for an analytical technique that enables researchers to shift their analytical focus from the detail of local contexts, different stakeholders' interactions, and different timelines to the broader global phenomenon that is constructed within these contexts, interactions, and timelines.[6] For instance, we zoomed into different local contexts to understand how specific PGEs and their stakeholders deal with local protection gaps. We also zoomed into the different, often contradictory, understandings, interests, and objectives that different stakeholders have (e.g., insurance industry vs government stakeholders). Finally, we zoomed into different time periods in the evolution of PGEs, both retrospectively and within the time we conducted our study.

We also "zoomed between" contexts, stakeholders, and time periods. We discussed the connections between these parts of the protection gap landscape. Our aim was to understand their interdependencies and how they shaped both local action within PGEs, and also the way the concept of the protection gap itself and the role of the insurance industry in disaster protection was evolving. For example, we developed patterns of how PGEs originate (Chapter 2) and evolve (Chapter 4), as well as how resilience is critical in addressing the protection gap (Chapter 5). Zooming in, zooming between, and zooming out enabled us to understand PGEs and their stakeholders as an interdependent global system dealing with a global issue.

A note on quality

The methodology underpinning this book has been through several processes that have helped build its quality. First, we engaged closely with and got feedback from our participants. For instance, we developed an industry report and presented it at industry events to validate our findings with participants.[7] Also, going back to the field after our initial analysis gave us a chance to "test" our emerging patterns to see if they held across our dataset and whether alternative patterns or explanations were at play. Second, as a research team, we engaged in constant team discussion and sharing of memos we made while collecting and analyzing our data.[8] Third, we involved different research assistants in coding our dataset, each of whom worked closely with the team, but at the same time acted as outsiders as they did not know the context and did not collect the data.

Notes

1. E.g., Elliott, R., *Underwater: Loss, Flood Insurance, and the Moral Economy of Climate Change in the United States.* New York: Columbia University Press; 2021.
2. Bruggeman, V., Faure, M. G., Fiore, K., "The Government as Reinsurer of Catastrophe Risks?" *The Geneva Papers on Risk and Insurance-Issues and Practice*, 35(3) (2010): 369–90. https://doi.org/10.1057/gpp.2010.10

3. McAneney, J., McAneney, D., Musulin, R., Walker, G., Crompton, R., "Government-Sponsored Natural Disaster Insurance Pools: A View from Down-Under." *International Journal of Disaster Risk Reduction*, 15 (2016): 1–9. https://doi.org/10.1016/j.ijdrr.2015.11.004.

Bruggeman et al., "The Government as Reinsurer."

4. Lampel, J., Meyer, A. D., "Field-Configuring Events as Structuring Mechanisms: How Conferences, Ceremonies, and Trade Shows Constitute New Technologies, Industries, and Markets." *Journal of Management Studies*, 45(6) (2008): 1025–35. http://dx.doi.org/10.1111/j.1467-6486.2008.00787.x

5. Lê, J. K., Schmid, T., "The Practice of Innovating Research Methods." *Organizational Research Methods*, 25(2) (2022): 308–36. https://doi.org/10.1177/1094428120935498.

Pratt, M. G., Sonenshein, S., Feldman, M. S., "Moving beyond Templates: A Bricolage Approach to Conducting Trustworthy Qualitative Research." *Organizational Research Methods*, 25(2) (2022): 211–28. https://doi.org/10.1177/1094428120927466

6. Nicolini, D., *Practice Theory, Work and Organization*. Oxford: Oxford University Press, 2012.

7. Lincoln, Y. S., Guba, E. G., "But is it Rigorous? Trustworthiness and Authenticity in Naturalistic Evaluation." *New Directions for Program Evaluation*, 30 (1986): 73–84. https://doi.org/10.1002/ev.1427

8. Jarzabkowski, P., Bednarek, R., Cabantous, L., "Conducting Global Team-Based Ethnography: Methodological Challenges and Practical Methods." *Human Relations*, 68(1) (2015): 3–33. https://doi.org/10.1177/0018726714535449

Glossary

Organizations

ARC (African Risk Capacity) was established in 2012 as a Specialized Agency of the African Union (AU), with 18 Member States that signed the Establishment Agreement initially, which has grown to 35 Member States in 2022. ARC aims to provide insurance products that help protect food security in the face of extreme weather disasters, such as drought.

ARPC (Australian Reinsurance Pool Corporation) is a corporate Commonwealth entity established in 2003 that provides reinsurance cover for property terrorism risk in Australia.

CEA (California Earthquake Authority) is a not-for-profit, publicly managed, privately funded entity established in 1996 that provides insurance cover against earthquake in California, USA.

CCR (Caisse Centrale de Réassurance/Central Reinsurance Fund) is a public-sector reinsurer established in 1946 that provides insurers operating in France with coverage against multiple "natural" disasters and other risks.

CCRIF SPC (Caribbean Catastrophe Risk Insurance Facility) is an entity established in 2007 that provides insurance cover for hurricane, earthquake, and excess rainfall to its members. As of 2022, CCRIF has 22 members, 19 Caribbean government members and three Central American government members.

Consorcio (Consorcio de Compensación de Seguros/Insurance Compensation Consortium) is a state-owned entity established in 1941 that provides insurance cover for "natural" and terrorism disasters in Spain.

EQC (Earthquake Commission) is a public entity established in 1945 that provides insurance to residential property owners against earthquake and associated disasters such as natural landslip, volcanic eruption, and hydrothermal activity in New Zealand. In 2022 it was renamed Toka Tū Ake EQC.

Flood Re is a reinsurance pool established in 2016 to provide insurance cover against flood in the UK.

FONDEN (Fideicomiso Fondo de Desastres Naturales/Trust Fund for Natural Disasters), now closed, was created in 1996 at the national level in Mexico to increase the Mexican Federal Government's resources and means for rehabilitation and reconstruction of public infrastructure, low-income housing, and certain components of the natural environment in the aftermath of disasters.

GAREAT (Gestion de l'Assurance et de la Réassurance des risques Attentats et actes de Terrorisme/Management of the Insurance and Reinsurance of Risks of Terrorist Attacks and Acts of Terrorism) is a private-public partnership established in 2002 that provides reinsurance cover against terrorism in France.

NFIP (National Flood Insurance Program) is a scheme established in 1968 in the US, that provides flood insurance to property owners, renters, and businesses, and works with communities required to adopt and enforce flood-plain management regulations that help mitigate flooding effects.

PCRIC (Pacific Catastrophe Risk Insurance Company) is an entity established in 2016 that is owned by the Pacific Catastrophe Risk Insurance Foundation (PCRIF) which is directed by the participating Pacific Island Countries to provide disaster risk finance products against natural and climatic disasters to Pacific Island countries. The aim is to provide liquidity to the participating countries as quickly as possible after a disaster. As of 2022 there are six members of PCRFI.

PEF (Pandemic Emergency Financing Facility) was a financing scheme, now closed, designed to provide an additional source of financing to help the world's poorest countries respond to cross-border, large-scale pandemic outbreaks.

Pool Re is a reinsurance pool established in 1993 to provide reinsurance cover against terrorism in the UK.

SASRIA (South African Special Risk Association) is an insurance company established in 1973 to provide cover for damage caused by special risks such as politically motivated malicious acts, riots, strikes, terrorism and public disorder.

Swiss system (KGV) is the cantonal level public-sector building insurers known as Kantonale Gebäudeversicherungen (KGVs) that provide disaster insurance. The KGVs operate in parallel with a private insurance system for disaster losses.

TCIP (Turkish Catastrophe Insurance Pool) is an insurance pool established in 2000 that enables affordable insurance premiums for homeowners in Turkey by sharing risk across the country without reverting to government budget. The pool is now expanding and is expected to provide insurance coverage against floods, landslides, storms, hail, frost, avalanches, and other disasters.

TRIA (Terrorism Risk Insurance Act) is a scheme established in the aftermath of the September 11, 2001 USA terrorist attacks, to ensure ongoing availability of terrorism insurance in the USA. The Act, through the Terrorism Risk Insurance Program, allows insurers to offer terrorism insurance policies, backed by a government guarantee to pay any claims, with those claims to be recouped from the insurance industry after a loss.

Terminology

Anticipatory financing[1] is a form of financing for which the capital has been put in place before the anticipated trigger of a payout. For instance, insurance is an anticipatory financing mechanism as the capital for reconstruction post-disaster has been put in place before the disaster happens.

Business interruption insurance covers a business for loss of income during periods when they cannot carry out business as usual due to damage caused by a specific set of disasters that will be specified in the policy. Traditional business interruption insurance covered mainly property damage. However, business interruption can happen without real property damage. This is known as "non-damage business interruption." Examples can include a cyber-attack or an extreme weather disaster that could cause disruptions and increased cost of working for businesses.

Disasters are large-scale catastrophes that cause great damage or loss of life. Examples include earthquakes, hurricanes, floods, terrorist attacks, and pandemics. Two houses being flooded is not a disaster; a town under water is.

Disaster insurance (sometimes called catastrophe insurance) refers to insurance of relatively low-frequency disasters with the potential for above-average or severe losses.

Disaster liquidity is the short-term cash flow (liquidity) necessary in the aftermath of disasters to start recovery efforts while maintaining essential government services.

Disaster-response protection gap is a gap between the need for rapid liquidity to respond to a disaster and the ability of the government of such countries to meet the costs of that liquidity themselves.

Disequilibrium is a conceptual term referring to the imbalance within and between the three paradoxes of insurability—the knowledge, control, and responsibility paradoxes (see *paradox*)—which means that some disaster can no longer be insured within the traditional private-sector risk transfer process. It is the counter situation to *(dynamic) equilibrium.*

(Dynamic) equilibrium[2] means continuous balancing within and between the three paradoxes of insurability—the knowledge, control, and responsibility paradoxes (see *paradox*). Any ongoing imbalance between them might push some disaster risk out of the insurability zone. We define that as *disequilibrium.*

Event is an insurance industry term meaning a disaster that has caused insured losses. We sometimes use this term where it is the most appropriate term in relation to the context.

(Risk) exposure refers to the inventory of elements such as citizens, infrastructure, housing, production capacities and other tangible human assets in an area in which disasters may occur. Measures of exposure can include the number of citizens or types of assets in an area.

Financial resilience is the financial capacity of governments, private sector, and citizens to respond to and recover from disaster through insurance-based mechanisms.

Insurance protection gap is the gap between the insured and actual economic losses caused by large-scale catastrophic disasters. It is generally used to refer to a global problem, affecting all countries, and referring to the whole uninsured population, but can also be used to explain the gap between insured and economic loss for specific countries and regions, or for specific disasters.

Levy in insurance is an amount of money, in the form of a compulsory fee or premium, that is imposed on insurance companies and/or policyholders.

Marketization occurs when activities that are important for society, such as education, health care, or protection from disaster, are provided through a market. This is the foundation for understanding that risks can be defined, evaluated, and traded to generate profit.[3]

Model (modeling, risk-modeling) refers to the tools and analytical approach to assessing risk that has been formulated within a relatively standardized set of statistical parameters. Modeling is a primary way that insurance knowledge about risk has been built and increased in recent years. Most disaster models comprise assessment of the particular disaster, the exposure to that disaster (see *exposure*), and the vulnerability (see *vulnerability*) to damage of the assets exposed to the forces generated by that disaster.

Moral hazard refers to the problem of policyholders, particularly those at the highest risk of repeated loss, not being incentivized to reduce their risk, or change risky behaviors (e.g., through structural changes to their property to mitigate the effects of flood) since other parties (insurers and/or PGEs and government) will incur the cost.

Multi-country risk pool is a pool of multiple countries coming together to gain some form of insurance protection. Such pools constitute a collective pot of operating capital, administrative and modeling capability, and geographic spread of risk that enables each country to buy a disaster liquidity insurance product that is underwritten by the global reinsurance industry.

Paradox means contradictory but interdependent elements. The interdependent nature of the contradictory forces means they are persistent (rather than resolvable) tensions.[4] This book looks at three such paradoxes that define insurability.

- Paradox (control) The *control paradox* is a tension between the extent to which the private insurance industry or the government controls how the market provides protection to society.

- Paradox (knowledge) The *knowledge paradox* relates to the tension between too little and too much knowledge about the risk of loss; disasters are insurable when they sit between enough knowledge to model and price for the potential losses, but not so much knowledge that how often the loss will occur and to whom, is a certainty.

- Paradox (responsibility) The *responsibility paradox* relates to the tensions between individual policyholders taking responsibility for their potential to incur losses to the collective pool of policyholders, as that collective pool takes responsibility to pay for losses to any individuals within it.

Parametric insurance is a type of insurance that uses a parameter or an index of parameters of a particular disaster as triggers for issuing a payout. Such insurance products may combine a mix of triggers from indemnity to industry loss, to the occurrence of specific parameters of a disaster, such as wind speeds within a specified zone. Parametric products can also be linked to modeled losses (as opposed to actual claims for losses), triggering a payment when losses exceed a particular threshold.

Physical resilience in this book refers to pre-disaster mitigation efforts with properties, infrastructure, and the environment, such as changing where and how assets and infrastructure are built, to make them less prone to losses from a disaster and/or enable their more rapid recovery from a disaster (see *resilient reconstruction*).

Premium is the amount of money an individual or business pays for an insurance policy.

Preparedness is the development of early warning systems, support of emergency measures, and contingency planning to prepare for disasters.

Protection gap (global) is the gap between the insured and actual economic losses caused by large-scale disasters (see *insurance protection gap*).

Protection gap (local) refers to specific gaps between insured and economic loss in a particular region, such as lack of terrorism cover for city-center business districts; insufficient emergency capital reserves in developing economies to maintain essential services after natural disaster; or unaffordable premiums for homeowners in highly exposed flood plains, or in earthquake-prone regions.

Protection Gap Entity (PGE) is the entity that brings together different market and non-market stakeholders to address the protection gap by transforming uninsured risk into insurance-based products that can be transferred onto government balance sheets or into global financial markets to provide capital for recovery following a disaster. They are thus not-for-profit entities, sitting at the intersection between public-sector and private-sector interests in insurance. While most PGEs exist within a specific country or state, some PGEs span multiple countries (see multi-country risk pools).

Reinsurer is a firm that supplies capital to pay for potential losses to an insurer. The insurer transfers the risk of a loss to the reinsurer, who holds capital in reserve to pay for such losses, in return for which the reinsurer receives a premium from the insurer (see Appendix A).

Resilient reconstruction is the reconstruction of property and other assets after a disaster to make them more physically resilient to future disasters (see *physical resilience*).

Risk is the possibility of loss.

Risk identification is building the capacity to identify, assess, and analyze risk, typically as a technical capability supporting the quantification of risk assessments and risk communication.

Risk mitigation refers to taking action prior to disaster to reduce the adverse effects of disasters.

Risk redistribution refers to the market intervention of taking the risk of loss by a relatively small group of policyholders that live in areas highly exposed to disaster and redistributing it across the wider pool of variably exposed policyholders. It is typically used in situations where risk-reflective pricing makes insurance unaffordable for policyholders in highly exposed areas.

Risk-reflective pricing is the actuarial practice of charging premiums to policyholders according to the risk they bear. That means that policyholders that are at higher risk of disaster are charged proportionally a higher premium from those that are at lower risk of disaster.

Risk removal refers to a market intervention in which risk is removed from the market onto the balance sheet of the PGE or the government. Risk removal is particularly likely for risk that is seen as too volatile or extreme for the insurance industry to take, such as terrorism.

Uninsurable risk refers to risk for which insurance is either unavailable from insurers (not offered) and/or unaffordable for policyholders (not bought due to high premiums)

Vulnerability refers to the propensity of exposed elements such as individuals, a community, and assets to suffer adverse effects from disasters.

Notes

1. Surminski, S., "Insurance Instruments for Climate-Resilient Development." In Fankhauser, S., McDermott, T. K. J., eds, *The Economics of Climate-Resilient Development*. Cheltenham: Edward Elgar Publishing, 2016, chapter 10. https://doi.org/10.4337/9781785360312.00020
2. Smith, W. K., Lewis, M. W., "Toward a Theory of Paradox: A Dynamic Equilibrium Model of Organizing." *Academy of Management Review*, 36(2) (2011): 381–403. https://doi.org/10.5465/amr.2009.0223

3. Callon, M., "Revisiting Marketization: From Interface-Markets to Market-Agencements." *Consumption Markets and Culture*, 19(1) (2016): 17–37. https://doi.org/10.1080/10253866.2015.1067002
4. Smith, Lewis, "Toward a Theory of Paradox."

Index